TARGUMIC TRADITIONS
AND THE NEW TESTAMENT

Society of Biblical Literature

===== *ARAMAIC STUDIES* =====

NUMBER 4

TARGUMIC TRADITIONS
AND THE NEW TESTAMENT
by
J.T. Forestell, C.S.B.

TARGUMIC TRADITIONS
AND THE NEW TESTAMENT
An Annotated Bibliography
with a New Testament Index

J. T. Forestell, C.S.B.

SCHOLARS PRESS

Distributed by
Scholars Press
101 Salem Street
PO Box 2268
Chico, California 95927

Targumic Traditions
and The New Testament

J.T. Forestell, C.S.B.

Library of Congress Cataloging in Publication Data

Forestell, J Terence.
 Targumic traditions and the New Testament.

 (Aramaic studies ; no. 4 ISSN 0145-2703)
 Includes indexes.
 1. Bible. O.T. Aramaic—Bibliography. 2. Bible.
N.T.—Criticism, interpretation, etc.—Bibliography. I. Title. II.
Series.
Z7772.A1F67 [BS709.4]   016.2206   79-19293
ISBN 0-89130-352-9

Printed in the United States of America
1   2   3   4   5
Edwards Brothers, Inc.
Ann Arbor, Michigan 48104

TABLE OF CONTENTS

ACKNOWLEDGEMENTS

This bibliography has been prepared with the help of a research grant from the Canada Council, Humanities and Social Sciences Division. The need for such a bibliography was suggested independently by Professor E. G. Clarke of the Department of Near Eastern Studies at the University of Toronto, and Professor R. Le Déaut C. S. Sp. of the Pontifical Biblical Institute, Rome. Special thanks are due to Professor Le Déaut for the generous assistance which he gave the author during a sabbatical leave in Rome during the academic year 1977-78. Nonetheless the author accepts full responsibility for all defects in the present work.

January 12, 1979   J. T. Forestell C.S.B.,
                                    St. Michael's College,
                                    Toronto, Canada

ABBREVIATIONS

Biblical Books

Gen	Hag	Matt
Exod	Zech	Mark
Lev	Mal	Luke
Num	Ps (Pss)	John
Deut	Job	Acts
Josh	Prov	Rom
Judg	Ruth	1-2 Cor
1-2 Sam	Cant	Gal
1-2 Kgs	Eccl	Eph
Isa	Lam	Phil
Jer	Esth	Col
Ezek	Dan	1-2 Thess
Hos	Ezra	1-2 Tim
Joel	Neh	Titus
Amos	1-2 Chr	Phlm
Obad	Jdt	Heb
Jonah	Sir	Jas
Mic	Tob	1-2 Pet
Nah	Wis	1-2-3 John
Hab	Bar	Jude
Zeph		Rev

Pseudepigrapha etc.

Adam and Eve	Books of Adam and Eve
2-3 Apoc. Bar.	Syriac, Greek Apocalypse of Baruch
4 Ezra	
Apoc. Mos.	Apocalypse of Moses
As. Mos.	Assumption of Moses
1-2-3 Enoch	Ethiopic, Slavonic, Hebrew Enoch
Ep. Arist.	Epistle of Aristeas
Jub.	Jubilees
Mart. Isa.	Martyrdom of Isaiah
Pss. Sol.	Psalms of Solomon
Sib. Or.	Sibylline Oracles
T. 12 Patr.	Testaments of the Twelve Patriarchs
T. Levi	Testament of Levi
T. Benj	Testament of Benjamin, etc.
Bib. Ant.	Ps.-Philo , Biblical Antiquities

Dead Sea Scrolls and Related Texts

CD	Cairo Geniza text of the Damascus Document
Ḥev	Naḥal Ḥever texts
Mas	Masada texts
Mird	Khirbet Mird texts
Mur	Wadi Murabba^cat texts
p	Pesher (commentary)
1Q, 2Q, 3Q, etc.	Numbered caves of Qumran yielding written material
1QapGen	*Genesis Apocryphon* of Qumran Cave I
1QH	*Hôdāyôt (Thanksgiving Hymns)* from Qumran Cave 1
1QpHab	*Pesher on Habakkuk* from Qumran Cave 1
1QM	*Milḥāmāh (War Scroll)*
1QS	*Serek hayyaḥad (Rule of the Community, Manual of Discipline)*
1QSa	Appendix A (*Rule of the Congregation*) to 1QS
1QSb	Appendix B (Blessings) to 1QS
11QMelch	*Melchizedek* text from Qumran Cave 11
11QtgJob	Targum of Job from Qumran Cave 11

Targumic Material (apart from Qumran material)

Tg. (Tgs.)	Targum (Targums)
Neof. (m., gl.)	Neofiti 1 (marginal glosses, interlinear glosses
Onq.	Targum Onqelos
Ps.-J.	Targum Pseudo-Jonathan
Frg. BLNPSV	Fragmentary Targum, Bomberg, Leningard 1, Nürnberg 1, Paris 110, Sassoon, Vatican 440.
Sam. Tg.	Samaritan Targum
Tg. Neb.	Targum of the Prophets
Tg. Ket.	Targum of the Writings
Tg. Isa	Targum of Isaiah
Tg. 1 Chr	Targum of 1 Chronicles
Pal. Tgs.	Palestinian Targums
Tg. Esth I, II	First or Second Targum of Esther
CTg. ABCDE	Cairo Geniza material, Mss ABCDE

Rabbinic Literature

The abbreviations used are those proposed for use in the *Journal of Biblical Literature* 95 (1976) 331-46.

Periodicals and Series

AJBA	*Australian Journal of Biblical Archaeology*
ALUOS	Annual of Leeds University Oriental Society
AnBib	Analecta Biblica
ASNU	Acta Seminarii Neotestamentici Upsaliensis
AsSeign	*Assemblées du Seigneur*
AugRom	*Augustinianum* (Roma)
AusBR	*Australian Biblical Review*
BeO	*Bibbia e Oriente*
BETL	Bibliotheca Ephimeridum Theologicarum Lovaniensium
BFCT	Beiträge zur Förderung christlicher Theologie
Bib	*Biblica*
BJRL	*Bulletin of the John Rylands University Library. of Manchester*
BTB	*Biblical Theology Bulletin*
BZ	*Biblische Zeitschrift*
BZAW	Beihefte zur *Zeitschrift für die alttestamentliche Wissenschaft*
BZNW	Beihefte zur *Zeitschrift für die neutestamentliche Wissenschaft*
CBQ	*Catholic Biblical Quarterly*
ConB	Coniectanea Biblica
ConNT	*Coniectanea Neotestamentica*
CuBib	*Cultura Bíblica*
DBSup	*Dictionnaire de la Bible. Supplément*
EstBib	*Estudios Bíblicos*
EstE	*Estudios Eclesiásticos*
ETL	*Ephemerides Theologicae Lovanienses*
ETR	*Etudes théologiques et religieuses*
EuntDoc	*Euntes Docentes*
EvQ	*Evangelical Quarterly*
ExpTim	*Expository Times*
HibJ	*Hibbert Journal*
HTR	*Harvard Theological Review*
HUCA	*Hebrew Union College Annual*
Int	*Interpretation*
ITQ	*Irish Theological Quarterly*
JAOS	*Journal of the American Oriental Society*
JBL	*Journal of Biblical Literature*
JBR	*Journal of Bible and Religion*
JJS	*Journal of Jewish Studies*
JNES	*Journal of Near Eastern Studies*
JQR	*Jewish Quarterly Review*

JR	Journal of Religion
JSJ	Journal for the Study of Judaism in the Persian, Hellenistic and Roman Period
JSS	Journal of Semitic Studies
JTS	Journal of Theological Studies
LD	Lectio Divina
LTK	Lexikon für Theologie und Kirche
Mar	Marianum
NCE	M. R. P. McGuire et al (eds.), New Catholic Encyclopedia
NovT	Novum Testamentum
NovTSup	Novum Testamentum, Supplements
NTS	New Testament Studies
OrAnt	Oriens Antiquus
RB	Revue Biblique
RechBib	Recherches Bibliques
REJ	Revue des Etudes juives
RevScRel	Revue des Sciences religieuses
RHPR	Revue d'Histoire et de Philosophie religieuses
RivB	Rivista Biblica
RQ	Revue de Qumrân
RSR	Recherches de Science religieuse
Salmant	Salmanticensis
SANT	Studien zum Alten und Neuen Testament
SB	Sources Bibliques
SBFLA	Studii biblici franciscani liber annuus
SBLMS	Society of Biblical Literature Monograph Series
SC	Sources Chrétiennes
Scr	Scripture
SEÅ	Svensk Exegetisk Årsbok
Sef	Sefarad
Sem	Semitica
SJLA	Studies in Judaism in Late Antiquity
SNTSMS	Society for New Testament Studies Monograph Series
SPap	Studia papyrologica
SPB	Studia postbiblica
SR	Studies in Religion/Sciences religieuses
ST	Studia theologica
TBT	The Bible Today
TerSa	Terra Santa
TLZ	Theologische Literaturzeitung
TRu	Theologische Rundschau
TZ	Theologische Zeitschrift

VD	*Verbum Domini*
VT	*Vetus Testamentum*
VTSup	Vetus Testamentum Supplements
WTJ	*Westminster Theological Journal*
WUNT	Wissenschaftliche Untersuchungen zum Neuen Testament
ZDMG	*Zeitschrift der deutschen morgenländischen Gesellschaft*
ZNW	*Zeitschrift für die neutestamentliche Wissenschaft*
ZTK	*Zeitschrift für Theologie und Kirche*

INTRODUCTION

In recent years there has been a renewed interest among
scholars, Jewish and Christian alike, in the Aramaic versions of
the Law, the Prophets, and the Writings, commonly called Targums.
In 1956 Alejandro Díez Macho identified the Vatican Ms. Neofiti 1
as a complete Palestinian Targum of the Pentateuch.[1] Paul Kahle's
publication of Cairo Geniza fragments in 1930[2] had already
furnished serious grounds for believing that a complete Palestinian
Targum of the Pentateuch existed, prior to the Mishna and the
universal acceptance of the official Targums of the Law and the
Prophets, commonly known as Onqelos and Jonathan respectively.[3]
This complete Palestinian Targum of the Pentateuch now appears to
be represented by Neofiti 1, in spite of the outstanding problems
concerning the later revision of the traditions contained in this
manuscript. Finally, the discovery of Targums of Job and Leviticus
at Qumran[4] provided the long-desired evidence that written Targums
were known in the pre-Christian era, even though the Qumran material
derived from a sectarian and esoteric group.

Parallel to these discoveries, a new interest was developing
in the history of Jewish biblical exegesis, especially in the
methods of midrashic interpretation. The pioneer work of A.
Robert[5] and R. Bloch[6] was already showing that the process of
re-interpretation and adaptation of older texts had begun in the
Old Testament itself and continued throughout the post-biblical
period into the rabbinic period. This midrashic process produced
the great monuments of rabbinic literature--the Mishna, the
Tosepta, the two Talmuds, and the Midrashim--and continued to
influence Jewish exegesis into the Middle Ages. R. Bloch had
already proposed a method for tracing Jewish exegetical tradition
from the earliest texts of the Old Testament itself to the
medieval commentaries of Rashi[7], when she met her tragic death.
Subsequent scholars have refined her method and applied it to other
traditions.[8]

These developments have been responsible for a remarkable
increase of new publications concerning the origins and dating of
the Targums themselves and of the biblical interpretations contained
therein.[9] The interrelationship of the extant Targums is being

re-examined[10] and the need for new editions is being met.[11] The
new developments have also reopened the entire question of the
history, grammar, and lexicography of the Aramaic language, a
question which had practically lain dormant since the major works
of Gustaf Dalman.[12]

Interest in targumic studies, however, has not been confined
to Old Testament scholars, to Aramaists, and to the historians of
Judaism. New Testament scholars have always been interested in
the use made of the Old Testament by New Testament writers. Many
books and articles have appeared concerning the Old Testament text
used by New Testament writers in their citations and allusions.[13]
It has always been agreed that a better knowledge of Jewish exegesis
at the time of Christ would be an invaluable asset to the understanding of the New Testament. The use of rabbinic literature for
this purpose has always been precarious; for although much of
rabbinic teaching was early in origin, it was not committed to
writing prior to the third century of the Christian era.[14] The
precise effect of the destruction of Jerusalem in 70 A.D. upon
the character of Judaism has yet to be adequately assessed.
Consequently, the New Testament scholar could never be certain to
what extent the biblical interpretations of classical rabbinic
literature were commonly known throughout the first century A. D.
The Apocrypha and Pseudepigrapha were largely sectarian in
character and the actual range of their circulation was entirely
unknown. The works of Flavius Josephus were apologetic in
character and his historical reliability suspect. Philo lived and
wrote in Alexandria. His work was clearly hellenistic and its
relationship with Palestinian Judaism highly conjectural. This
lacuna in our knowledge of Jewish exegesis was partially filled
by the discovery of the Qumran literature, especially the *pešer*
commentaries on the various books of the Old Testament. This
literature has been abundantly used by New Testament scholarship.[15]
Nevertheless, although it has the distinct advantage of being
contemporary, it remains sectarian and esoteric. It cannot be
considered to be representative of Palestinian Judaism in the
first century of the Christian era.

Prior to Kahle's work, the Targums had been generally ignored
as a witness to Jewish exegesis in the first century A. D. Onqelos
and Jonathan were considered to be late and Babylonian in origin;
Pseudo-Jonathan showed dependence on Onqelos; the Fragmentary
Targum was incomplete and its date unknown. Some of the manuscripts
from the Cairo Geniza published in 1930 were dated by Kahle as
early as the seventh century A. D. and exhibited a text which was

similar in character to the so-called Fragmentary Targum. The
identification of Neofiti l by Díez Macho confirmed the existence
of a complete Palestinian Targum of the Pentateuch, which would
have been used in Palestine prior to the universal acceptance of
Onqelos about the tenth century. Nonetheless, subsequent scholarship has shown that we cannot speak of a standardized Palestinian
Targum of the Pentateuch, but must recognize that we are dealing
with a fluid tradition which was never given a unified form in
Palestine as it was in Babylon.

We know that the practice of translating the Hebrew Scriptures
into Aramaic in the synagogues is pre-Christian in origin and may
go back to the time of Ezra.[16] There certainly was an oral
targumic tradition in first century Palestine. Such a tradition
would be commonly known to all Jews who frequented the synagogue.
It is still a matter of conjecture to what extent this oral
tradition was already committed to writing in the pre-Christian
era. The discoveries at Qumran have proven that written Targums
did exist, but the relationship of Qumran with the synagogue remains
unknown. Nonetheless, using the methodology developed by R. Bloch
and refined by subsequent scholarship, it is possible to acknowledge
a pre-Christian or first century date for some of the traditions
contained in the Palestinian Targums. The same may be said for
traditions contained in Onqelos and Jonathan, to the extent that
these Targums can be shown to be ultimately Palestinian in
origin.[17] Targumic traditions which are also reflected in other
Jewish literature prior to the end of the first century of the
Christian era were most likely widely known in the Palestine of
Jesus' day and to the New Testament writers.[18] Some of these same
traditions are reflected in the New Testament, although the New
Testament alone cannot be considered an adequate witness to the
popular character of a targumic tradition.

The studies of G. Vermès[19], P. Grelot[20], S. Lyonnet[21], the
major work of R. Le Déaut[22], and the synthetic work of M.
McNamara[23] have established the place of targumic studies in
contemporary New Testament exegesis on a solid foundation. Other
scholars have followed in their footsteps and the methodology will
be further refined as our knowledge of the Targums themselves
improves. In spite of the problems which still exist, the New
Testament exegete can no longer afford to ignore these new
developments in contemporary scholarship.[24]

Targumic studies have also had their influence upon other areas
of New Testament research. Three further questions have been
affected by recent developments. To what extent does the Aramaic

language of the Palestinian Targums reflect the language of first
century Palestine and the language of Jesus? The reservations of
J. Fitzmyer have at least indicated the necessity of further study
in this area.[25] May one legitimately use the Aramaic of the
Palestinian Targums to uncover the Aramaic substratum of the New
Testament, especially in the sayings of Jesus and the speeches of
Acts? What effect do targumic studies have upon New Testament
textual criticism, especially as regards the semitisms of Codex
Bezae and the earliest versions?[26] These latter questions are
much more problematic, since contemporary documentary evidence is
practically limited to the texts of Qumran and Murabba[c]at. These
documents exhibit a literary Aramaic which is still closer to
imperial Aramaic than to the Aramaic of the Palestinian Targums and
Talmud. The influence of spoken Aramaic is already apparent in
these texts, but there is still heated discussion concerning the
relationship of the Aramaic of the Palestinian Targums to the
spoken Aramaic of Jesus' day. Díez Macho is probably right,
however, when he insists on the inadequacy of merely orthographical
and syntactical considerations and invokes semantic considerations
as well.[27]

     In spite of the methodological and linguistic problems which
remain unresolved in this field of study, the New Testament scholar
can no longer afford to neglect the thought-provoking studies
which have been produced over the past twenty years. The bibliography of Peter Nickels, *Targum and New Testament. A Bibliography
together with a New Testament Index* (Rome: Pontifical Biblical
Institute, 1967) was a pioneer effort to provide New Testament
scholars with a useful tool for mining the riches of these new
discoveries. It is now over ten years old and much new work has
appeared in the meantime. It seems that the time is ripe for a
new bibliography which will not only complete Nickels' work, but
will also provide the New Testament scholar with more information
concerning studies in this field and a ready means of discovering
to what degree targumic studies have proven useful for New
Testament interpretation.
     The bibliography is intended to meet the needs of the New
Testament scholar rather than those of the librarian. Its scope
has therefore been restricted in such a way that this tool may not
only be as useful as possible, but also that it may be available
to scholars as soon as possible. New studies are always appearing
and subsequent work improves upon or supersedes older work. For

this reason, provision has been made for the individual scholar to
keep his own copy up to date. The bibliography will therefore be
restricted to significant work published since 1930--the date of
Kahle's *Masoreten des Westens II* and will concentrate on work
published since 1956--the date of Díez Macho's identification of
Neofiti 1. The first chapter of M. McNamara's study, *The New
Testament and the Palestinian Targum to the Pentateuch* (AnBib 27;
Rome: Pontifical Biblical Institute, 1966), provides the scholar
with an adequate bibliography of earlier work.[28]

The voluminous collection of Hermann Strack and Paul
Billerbeck, *Kommentar zum Neuen Testament aus Talmud und Midrasch*
(Vols. I-IV München: Beck, 1922-28); Vol. V: *Rabbinischer Index*
(edd. J. Jeremias, K. Adolph; München: Beck, 1956); Vol. VI:
Verzeichnis der Schriftgelehrten. Geographisches Register (edd.
J. Jeremias, K. Adolph; Munchen: Beck, 1961); reprint 1969,
includes many references to the Targums, but these are minimal
compared to the bulk of the whole. Frequently they simply provide
the Aramaic equivalent of Hebrew and Greek expressions in the Old
and New Testaments respectively. When they are significant for
the understanding of the text, they are buried in a mass of other
rabbinic material in such a way that their significance neither
stands out nor is developed. Many of the more significant references in Strack-Billerbeck have been taken up and developed more
critically by subsequent studies. The collection is already
organized according to chapter and verse of the New Testament
and is provided with an index of Targum references. Since scholars
will continue to use Strack-Billerbeck as a tool, it has seemed
unnecessary to incorporate its material into the present bibliography. Nonetheless, all New Testament scholars should heed the
salutary warnings of Samuel Sandmel[29] in using these volumes for
targumic and rabbinic material. In spite of the difficulties
involved, recourse to the original texts and contexts is a *sine
qua non* of responsible New Testament scholarship where Jewish
literature is concerned. Strack-Billerbeck can only provide a
first contact with the texts, and Billerbeck's translations and
interpretations must always be controlled against the original
texts themselves.

Although much was written concerning the New Testament and
rabbinic Judaism in the period between 1930-1956, little use was
made of targumic material.[30] From this period, therefore, only
those works which use the Targums explicitly for the elucidation
of New Testament texts have been included. Hence some works which
appeared in Nickels' bibliography will not be found in this work.

Much has also been written on the history and development of
midrashic exegesis in Judaism. The methods of targumic interpretation are midrashic in character and have frequently been used to
illustrate this history. While such studies are valuable in
themselves and provide a background for the interpretation of the
New Testament, a selection of the more important works has been
considered adequate for this bibliography. Those which make use
of New Testament illustrations have been preferred to those which
confine themselves to Jewish literature.

     The bibliography has, therefore, been divided into two parts:
Part I 1930-1955; Part II Since 1956. Within each section, books
and articles have been listed alphabetically, generally according
to the name of the author. When it has been considered advisable
to list entire *Festschriften*, they appear under the name of the
scholar to whom they are dedicated. Collected articles by a
variety of authors, when listed as monographs, are listed according
to the title of the volume. With most entries, brief annotations
indicate the major concerns or conclusions of the author. The
entries have been numbered in a continuous series of arabic
numerals. These numbers will be used in the New Testament index
for referring to the entries in the bibliography.
     Given the abundance of new literature in this field, it is
difficult to compile a useful New Testament index. The Targums
have been used to elucidate the New Testament interpretation of
Old Testament texts, New Testament midrashic exegesis, the
semantics of New Testament language, and finally New Testament
textual criticism. Moreover, the conclusions of earlier studies
are repeated and used in later works, with or without corrections
or modifications. Many surveys have appeared which simply repeat
everything that has already been accomplished. In other cases,
authors have suggested a great variety of New Testament texts
whose interpretation might be elucidated by targumic material,
without developing these suggestions in any substantial way.
Other studies which develop a theme from the Targums and Midrashim
are helpful in understanding some aspect of New Testament theology
which may appear in a variety of texts, e.g. the Akedah and New
Testament theology of redemption. It has been judged advisable,
therefore, to itemize only those New Testament texts whose
interpretation has been substantially affected by recourse to

targumic traditions. Once again, this decision will entail the
omission of some of the material contained in Nickels' New
Testament index. A brief annotation will generally indicate the
precise manner in which the text has been elucidated by the Targums.
The significant items of the bibliography will then be indicated
by numerical reference alone, followed by page numbers whenever
necessary. E.g. Eph 4:8: Ps 68:19 cited according to Tg.--259,
504-05; 267, 78-81 = S. Lyonnet, "St. Paul et l'exégèse juive de
son temps. A propos de Rom., 10, 6-8," *Mélanges...Robert* (1957)
494-506;M. McNamara, *The New Testament and the Palestinian Targum
to the Pentateuch* (1966)   78-81 OR John 1:1: Memra of Tgs. and
Logos of John--18; 286 = V. Hamp, *Der Begriff 'Wort' in den
aramäischen Bibelübersetzungen* (1938); D. Muñoz León, *Dios Palabra*
(1974). Reference will be made to substantive contributions but
not necessarily to all repetitions.

Finally, a short subject index will indicate New Testament
themes which have been substantially illuminated by targumic
studies. References to the bibliography will be made as in the
New Testament index. An appendix will list the latest publications
of Targum texts and fragments.

INTRODUCTION

[1]A. Díez Macho, "Una copia de todo el Targum jerosolimitano en la Vaticana," *EstBib* 15 (1956) 446-47; "Una copia completa del Targum palestinense al Pentateucho en la Bibliotheca vaticana," *Sef* 17 (1957) 119-21; "The Palestinian Targum," *Christian News from Israel* 13 (2, 1962) 19-25; "The Recently Discovered Palestinian Targum: Its Antiquity and Relationship with the other Targums," VTSup 7 (Congress Volume; Leiden: Brill, 1960) 222-45; "Magister-Minister, Professor P. E. Kahle through Twelve Years of Correspondence," *Recent Progress in Biblical Scholarship* (The Richard Kronstein Foundation; For Lincoln Lodge Research Library; Oxford: Boars Hill, 1965) 13-61. M. Black, "The Recovery of the Language of Jesus," *NTS* 3 (1957) 305-13.

[2]*Masoreten des Westens II* (Stuttgart: Kohlhammer, 1930; reprint Hildesheim: Olms, 1967).

[3]Cf. P. Kahle, *The Cairo Geniza* (Schweich Lectures 1941; London: Oxford University Press, 1947; 2nd ed. Oxford: Blackwell, 1959); German translation: *Die Kairoer Genisa. Untersuchungen zur Geschichte des hebräischen Bibeltextes und seiner Übersetzungen* (Berlin: Akademie Verlag, 1962); "Das zur Zeit Jesu in Palästina gesprochene Aramäisch," *TRu* 17 (1949) 201-16 = *Opera Minora* (Leiden: Brill, 1956) 79-95; "Das palästinische Pentateuchtargum und das zur Zeit Jesu gesprochene Aramäisch," *ZNW* 49 (1958) 100-16.

[4]*Le Targum de Job de la grotte XI de Qumrân.* Edité et traduit par J. Van der Ploeg et A. Van der Woude (Koninklijke Nederlandse Akademie van Wetenschaffen; Leiden: Brill, 1971). *Discoveries in the Judean Desert VI.* Qumrân Grotte 4 II. I. Archéologie par R. de Vaux avec les contributions de J. W. B. Barns et J. Carswell. II. Tefillin, Mezuzot et Targums (4Q128--4Q157) par J. T. Milik (Oxford: Clarendon, 1977) pp. 86-90.

[5]"Littéraires (Genres)," *DBSup* V 405-21 (Paris: Letouzey et Ané, 1957); "Les attaches littéraires bibliques de Proverbes I--IX," *RB* 43 (1934) 42-68; 172-204; 374-84; 44 (1935) 502-25. Cf. also A. Gelin, *Problèmes d'Ancien Testament* (Lyon: Vitte, 1952) 93-110 = "Comment le peuple d'Israël lisait l'Ancien Testament," *Rencontres* 35 (Paris: Cerf, 1951) 117-31.

[6]"Ecriture et tradition dans le judaïsme. Apercus sur l'origine du midrash," *Cahiers Sioniens* 8 (1954) 9-34; "Ezéchiel XVI: exemple parfait du procédé midrashique dans la Bible," *Cahiers Sioniens* 9 (1955) 193-223. Cf. also M. Gertner, "Midrashim in the New Testament," *JSS* 7 (1962) 267-92. R. Le Déaut, "A propos d'une définition du midrash," *Bib* 50 (1969) 395-413 = "Apropos a Definition of Midrash," *Int* 25 (1971) 259-82. G. Vermés, "Bible and Midrash: Early Old Testament Exegesis," *The Cambridge History of the Bible* I 199-231 (Cambridge: University Press, 1970).

[7]"Note méthodologique pour l'étude de la littérature rabbinique," *RSR* 43 (1955) 194-227. For earlier suggestions concerning such a methodology, cf. A. Wikgren, "The Targums and the New Testament,"

JR 24 (1944) 89-95. G. D. Kilpatrick, *The Origin of the Gospel according to St. Matthew* (Oxford: Clarendon, 1946). P. Winter, "Lc 2,49 and Targum Jerushalmi," *ZNW* 45 (1954) 145-79.

[8]Cf. esp. G. Vermès, *Scripture and Tradition in Judaism. Haggadic Studies* (SPB 4; Leiden: Brill, 1961; 2nd ed. 1973); *Post-Biblical Jewish Studies* (SJLA 8; Leiden: Brill, 1975). P. Grelot, "L'exégèse messianique d'Isaïe LXIII, 1-6," *RB* 70 (1963) 371-80. R. Le Déaut, *La Nuit Pascale. Essai sur la signification de la Pâque juive à partir du Targum d'Exode XII 42* (AnBib 22; Rome: Institut Biblique Pontifical, 1963; reprint 1975), and his numerous other studies. M. McNamara, *The New Testament and the Palestinian Targum to the Pentateuch* (AnBib 27; Rome: Pontifical Biblical Institute, 1966). M. Miller, "Targum, Midrash and the Use of the Old Testament in the New Testament," *JSJ* 2 (1971) 29-82, with bibliographies.

[9]Besides the standard bibliographical tools, cf. B. Grossfeld, *A Bibliography of Targum Literature* (Bibliographica Judaica 38; 2 vols.; Cincinnati/New York: Hebrew Union College/Ktav, 1972-77). P. Nickels, *Targum and New Testament. A Bibliography together with a New Testament Index* (Rome: Pontifical Biblical Institute, 1967). W. E. Aufrecht (ed.), *Newsletter for Targumic and Cognate Studies* (Toronto: Victoria College, 1974-   ). Cf. also the extensive survey of bibliography in the introductions to the various volumes of the *editio princeps* of Neofiti 1, published at Madrid and Barcelona by the Consejo Superior de Investigaciones Científicas under the direction of A. Díez Macho.

[10]An abundant literature has been devoted to such questions. Among the more significant contributions, note the following: P. Kahle, "Das zur Zeit Jesu in Palästina gesprochene Aramäisch," *TRu* 17 (1949) 201-16 = *Opera Minora* (Leiden: Brill, 1956) 79-95. R. Bloch, "Note sur l'utilisation des fragments de la Geniza du Caire pour l'étude du Targum palestinien," *REJ* 114 (1955) 5-35. K. Bernhardt, "Zu Eigenart und Alter der messianisch-eschatologischen Zusätze im Targum Jeruschalmi I," *Gott und die Götter* (Festschrift E. Fascher; Berlin: Evangelische Verlagsanstalt, 1958) 68-83. P. Grelot, "Les Targums du Pentateuque. Etude comparative d'après Genèse, IV, 3-16," *Sem* 9 (1959) 59-88. A. Díez Macho, "En torno a la datación del Targum palestinense," *Sef* 20 (1960) 2-16; "The Recently Discovered Palestinian Targum: Its Antiquity and Relationship with the other Targums," VTSup 7 (Leiden: Brill, 1960) 222-45. P. Wernberg-Møller, "An Inquiry into the Validity of the Text-Critical Argument for an Early Dating of the Recently Discovered Palestinian Targum," *VT* 12 (1962) 312-30. A. M. Goldberg, "Die spezifische Verwendung des Terminus Schekhinah im Targum Onkelos als Kriterium einer relativen Datierung," *Judaica* 19 (1963) 43-61. G. Vermès, "Haggadah in the Onqelos Targum," *JSS* 8 (1963) 159-69 = *Post-Biblical Jewish Studies* (Leiden: Brill, 1975) 127-38. R. Le Déaut, *Introduction à la littérature targumique. Première partie* (ad usum privatum; Rome: Institut Biblique Pontifical, 1966). J.W. Bowker, "Haggadah in the Targum Onqelos," *JSS* 12 (1967) 51-65. M. Delcor, "La portée chronologique de quelques interprétations du Targoum Néophyti contenues dans le cycle d'Abraham," *JSJ* 1 (1970) 105-19. S. H. Levey, "The Date of the Targum Jonathan to the Prophets," *VT* 21 (1971) 186-96. B. Schaller, "Targum Jeruschalmi I zu Dt 33,11 ein Relikt aus hasmonäischer Zeit?" *JSJ* 3 (1972) 52-60. J. M. Sánchez Caro, "Las recensiones targumicas. Estudio de T. Deut. 1.1," *Salmant* 19 (1972) 605-34. S. A. Kaufman, "The Job Targum from Qumran," *JAOS* 93 (1973) 317-27. M. Ohana, "Agneau pascal et circoncision: le problème de la halakha prémishnaïque dans le Targum palestinien," *VT* 23 (1973) 385-99; "Prosélytisme et Targum palestinien: Données

nouvelles pour la datation de Néofiti 1," *Bib* 55 (1974) 317-32.
R. Le Déaut, "The Current State of Targumic Studies," *BTB* 4 (1974)
3-32. J. Heinemann, "Early Halakhah in the Palestinian Targumim,"
JJS 25 (1974) 114-22. A. York, "The Dating of the Targumic
Literature," *JSJ* 5 (1974) 49-62. G. J. Cowling, "Targum Neofiti,
Exodus 16:15," *AJBA* (1975) 93-105. R. Pummer, "The Present State
of Samaritan Studies," *JSS* 21 (1976) 39-61; 22 (1977) 27-47. C.
Perrot, "Le Targum," *ETR* 52 (1977) 219-30.

[11]
An appendix to the present bibliography lists recent editions of
the Targums. The most ambitious effort in this regard is the
preparation of the *Biblia Polyglotta Matritensis* under the direction
of A. Díez Macho with his team of scholars at the University of
Barcelona.

[12]E.g. *Grammatik des jüdisch palästinischen Aramäisch* (Leipzig:
Hinrichs, 1894; 2nd ed. 1905). *Aramäische Dialektproben* (Leipzig:
Hinrichs, 1896; 2nd ed. 1927). These studies have been reprinted
as one volume (Darmstadt: Wissenschaftliche Buchgesellschaft, 1960).
Die Worte Jesu (Leipzig: Hinrichs, 1898; 2nd ed. 1930). English
translation Edinburgh: T. & T. Clark, 1902. *Jesus-Jeschua. Die
drei Sprachen Jesu. Jesus in der Synagogue, auf dem Berge, beim
Passahmahl, am Kreuz* (=*Die Worte Jesu* Vol. II; Leipzig: Hinrichs,
1922; Erganzungen und Verbesserungen, 1929). English translation
London: SPCK, 1929.

[13]E.g. C. Smits, *Oud-testamentische citaten in het Nieuwe Testament*
4 vols. with French summaries (Collectanea Franciscana Neerlandica
VIII 1-4; 's-Hertogenbosch: Malmberg, 1952-63). K. Stendahl, *The
School of Matthew and its Use of the Old Testament* (ASNU 20;
Uppsala: Almqvist u. Wiksells, 1954; 2nd ed. 1968). J. W. Doeve,
Jewish Hermeneutics in the Synoptic Gospels and Acts (Assen: Van
Gorcum, 1954). E. E. Ellis, *Paul's Use of the Old Testament*
(Grand Rapids: Eerdmans, 1957). B. Lindars, *New Testament
Apologetics. The Doctrinal Significance of the Old Testament
Quotations* (London: SCM, 1961). E. D. Freed, *Old Testament Quota-
tions in the Gospel of John* (NovTSup 11; Leiden: Brill, 1965).
L. Hartman, *Prophecy Interpreted. The Formation of Some Jewish
Apocalyptic Texts and of the Eschatological Discourse. Mark 13
Par.* (ConNT 1; Lund: Gleerup, 1966). R. H. Gundry, *The Use of the
Old Testament in St. Matthew's Gospel. With Special Reference to
the Messianic Hope* (NovTSup 18; Leiden: Brill, 1967).

[14]Most recently, G. W. Buchanan, "The Use of Rabbinic Literature
for New Testament Research," *BTB* 7 (1977) 110-22. Cf. also G. F.
Moore, "Christian Writers on Judaism," *HTR* 14 (1921) 197-245. S.
Sandmel, "Parallelomania," *JBL* 81 (1962) 1-13. G. Vermès, "La
littérature rabbinique et le Nouveau Testament. Remarques
méthodologiques à propos de quelques livres récents," *Cahiers
Sioniens* 9 (1955) 97-123. M. Smith, "On the Problem of Method in
the Study of Rabbinic Literature," *JBL* 92 (1973) 112-13. For a
recent introduction to rabbinic literature, cf. J. Bowker, *The
Targums and Rabbinic Literature. An Introduction to Jewish
Interpretations of Scripture* (Cambridge: University Press, 1969).

[15]Cf. H. Braun, *Qumran und das Neue Testament* 2 vols. (Tubingen:
Mohr, 1966). G. Vermès, "Le 'Commentaire d'Habacuc' et le Nouveau
Testament," *Cahiers Sioniens* 5 (1951) 337-49; "The Qumran Interpre-
tation of Scripture in its Historical Setting," *Post-Biblical
Jewish Studies* (Leiden: Brill, 1975) 37-49; "The Impact of the Dead
Sea Scrolls on the Study of the New Testament," *JJS* 27 (1976)
107-16.

[16]Jewish tradition has seen the origin of the practice in Neh 8:8.
See the standard treatment in dictionaries, encyclopedias, and
introductions. T. Walker, "Targums," *Hastings Dictionary of the
Bible* IV 678-83 (Edinburgh: T. & T. Clark, 1898-1904). W. Bacher,
"Targums," *Jewish Encyclopedia* XII 57-63 (New York: Funk & Wagnalls,
1901-06). M. McNamara, "Bible, IV 11, Targums," *NCE* II 431-33
(New York: McGraw-Hill, 1967). V. Hamp, "Bibelübersetzungen III
(Jüdisch-) Aramäische B. od. Targumim," *LTK* II 384-86 (Freiburg:
Herder, 1958). B. Grossfeld, "Bible: Translations: Ancient
Versions. Aramaic: The Targumim," *Encyclopaedia Judaica* IV 841-
51 (Jerusalem: Keter, 1971). A. Díez Macho, "Targum," *Enciclopedia
de la Biblia* VI 865-81 (Barcelona: Garriga, 1963). A. Di Nola,
"Targumim," *Enciclopedia della Religioni* V 1645-57 (Firenze:
Vellechi, 1973). Díaz Fernández, J. R., "Targūm Samaritano,"
Enciclopedia de la Biblia VI 881-84 (Barcelona: Garriga, 1963).
B. J. Roberts, *The Old Testament Text and Versions* (Cardiff:
University of Wales, 1951) 197-213. Robert-Feuillet, *Introduction
à la Bible* I (Tournai: Desclée, 2nd ed. 1959) 90-95. O. Eissfeldt,
The Old Testament: An Introduction (Oxford: Blackwell, 1965) 696-
98. Sellin-Fohrer, *Einleitung in das Alte-Testament* (Heidelberg:
Quelle & Meyer, 10th ed. 1965) 556-57. A. Bentzen, *Introduction
to the Old Testament* (Copenhagen: Gad, 7th ed., reprint of 1952
2nd ed., 1967) I 68-72. G. Fohrer, *Introduction to the Old
Testament* (London: SPCK, 1970) 505-06. R. Le Déaut, "Targum,
midrash et exégèse juive ancienne," *Introduction à la Bible*.
Edition nouvelle Tome III. Introduction critique au Nouveau
Testament 1. Au seuil de l'ère chrétienne (edd. A. George, P.
Grelot; Paris: Desclée, 1976) 108-13. See also B. Gerhardsson,
*Memory and Manuscript. Oral Tradition and Written Transmission in
Rabbinic Judaism and Early Christianity* (Lund/Copenhagen: Gleerup/
Munksgaard, 1961; 2nd ed. 1964). P. Grelot, "Le Papyrus Pascal
d'Eléphantine: Essai de restauration," *VT* 17 (1967) 201-07. E.
Schürer, *The History of the Jewish People in the Age of Jesus
Christ* (175 B. C. -- A. D. 135). Revised edition by G. Vermès and
F. Millar, Vol. I (Edinburgh: T. & T. Clark, 1973) 99-114. P.S.
Alexander, "The Rabbinic Lists of Forbidden Targumim," *JJS* 27
(1976) 177-91.

[17]Recent studies by A. Tal and S. Kaufman have defended the Pales-
tinian origin of Onqelos and Jonathan; Kaufman would date the final
Palestinian form of these Targums between 70-135 A. D. Cf. R. Le
Déaut's review of A. Tal, *The Language of the Targum of the Former
Prophets and its Position within the Aramaic Dialects* (Tel Aviv:
Tel Aviv University, 1975) in *Bib* 58 (1977) 114.

[18]Not only the discovery of the targumic texts at Qumran, but also
traditions in the other Qumran literature with parallels in the
Targums indicate the importance of Qumran for targumic studies.
Cf. G. Vermès, "The Archangel Sariel. A Targumic Parallel to the
Dead Sea Scrolls," *Christianity, Judaism and Other Greco-Roman
Cults* (Studies for Morton Smith at Sixty: Part III: Judaism before
70; ed. J. Neusner; Leiden: Brill, 1975) 159-66; "A propos des
commentaires bibliques découverts à Qumrân," *RHPR* 35 (1955) 95-103.
G. R. Driver, *The Judaean Scrolls* (Oxford: Blackwell, 1965) 215,
456-57, 471-72.

[19]*Scripture and Tradition in Judaism. Haggadic Studies* (SPB 4:
Leiden: Brill, 1961; 2nd ed. 1973). *Post-Biblical Jewish Studies*
(SJLA 8; Leiden: Brill, 1975).

[20]"Les Targums du Pentateuque. Etude comparative d'après Genèse,
IV, 3-16," *Sem* 9 (1959) 59-88. "'De son ventre couleront des
fleuves d'eau'. La citation scripturaire de Jean VII, 38," *RB* 66

(1959) 369-74. "Le Messie dans les Apocryphes de l'Ancien
Testament. Etat de la question," *La Venue du Messie* (RechBib 6;
Bruges: Desclée de Brouwer, 1962) 19-50. "Jean, VII, 38: Eau du
rocher ou source du temple?" *RB* 70 (1963) 43-51. "L'exégèse
messianique d'Isaïe LXIII, 1-6," *RB* 70 (1963) 371-80.

[21]"Saint Paul et l'exégèse juive de son temps. A propos de Rom.,
10, 6-8," *Mélanges bibliques redigés en l'honneur d'André Robert*
(Paris: Bloud & Gay, 1957) 494-506. "L'histoire du salut selon le
chapitre VII de l'épître aux Romains," *Bib* 43 (1962) 117-51. "'Tu
ne convoiteras pas' (Rom. vii 7)," *Neotestamentica et Patristica*
(Festschrift O. Cullmann; Leiden: Brill, 1962) 157-65.

[22]*La Nuit Pascale. Essai sur la signification de la Pâque juive
à partir du Targum d'Exode XII 42* (AnBib 22; Rome: Institut
Biblique Pontifical, 1963; photographic reprint 1975), and many
other studies.

[23]*The New Testament and the Palestinian Targum to the Pentateuch*
(AnBib 27; Rome: Pontifical Biblical Institute, 1966). Cf. also
the more popular presentation, *Targum and Testament. Aramaic
Paraphrases of the Hebrew Bible. A Light on the New Testament*
(Grand Rapids/ Shannon: Eerdmans/Irish University Press, 1972).

[24]The significance of the Targums for NT interpretation was
perceived by a few scholars early in the century. Cf. H. St. J.
Thackeray, *The Relation of St. Paul to Contemporary Jewish Thought*
(London: Macmillan, 1900). E. A. Abbott, *Notes on New Testament
Criticism. Diatessarica* VII (London: A. & C. Black, 1907). R.
Harris, "Traces of Targumism in the New Testament," *ExpTim* 32
(1921) 373-76. M. Jousse, *Les formules targoûmiques du "Pater"
dans le milieu ethnique palestinien* (Paris: Geuthner, 1944). More
recently cf. P. Bonnati, C. Martini, *Il Messaggio della Salvezza I.
Introduzione Generale* (2nd ed. Torino/Leumann: Ella di Ci, 1966)
186-87. R. Le Déaut, "Tradition juive et exégèse chrétienne,"
*Jalones de la Historia de la Salvación en el Antiguo y Nuevo
Testamento* (26 Semana Biblica Española 1965; Madrid: CSIC, 1969)
II 7-33. M. McNamara, "The Aramaic Translations: A Newly Discovered
Aid for New Testament Study," *Scr* 18 (1966) 47-56 = *Irish Eccles-
iastical Record* 109 (1968) 158-65. G. J. Cowling, "New Light on the
New Testament? The Significance of the Palestinian Targum,"
Theological Students' Fellowship Bulletin 51 (1968) 6-14. E. E.
Ellis, "Midrash, Targum and New Testament Quotations," *Neotesta-
mentica et Semitica* (Festschrift M. Black; Edinburgh: T. & T.
Clark, 1969) 61-69. R. Le Déaut, "La tradition juive ancienne
et l'exégèse chrétienne primitive," *RHPR* 51 (1971) 31-50; "Un
phénomène spontané de l'herméneutique juive ancienne: le 'targuisme',"
Bib 52 (1971) 505-25; "Targumic Literature and New Testament Interpretation," *BTB* 4 (1974) 243-89; "Les targums ou versions araméenes
de la Bible," *SIDIC* 9 (2, 1976) 4-11. A. Paul, "Bulletin de
littérature intertestamentaire," *RSR* 60 (1972) 429-58.

[25]M. Black, "The Problem of the Aramaic Element in the Gospels,"
ExpTim 59 (1948) 171-76; "Die Erforschung der Muttersprache Jesu,"
TLZ 82 (1957) 653-68. W. Stinespring, "History and Present Status
of Aramaic Studies," *JBR* 26 (1958) 298-303. M. Smith, "Aramaic
Studies and the Study of the New Testament," *JBR* 26 (1958) 304-13.
P. Kahle, "Das palästinische Pentateuchtargum and das zur Zeit
Jesu gesprochene Aramäisch," *ZNW* 49 (1958) 100-16. A. Díez Macho,
"La Lengua hablada por Jesucristo," *OrAnt* 2 (1963) 95-132. H. Ott,
"Um die Muttersprache Jesu. Forschungen seit Gustaf Dalman,"
NovT 9 (1967) 1-25. H. P. Rüger, "Zum Problem der Sprache Jesu,"
ZNW 59 (1968) 113-22. J. Fitzmyer, "The Languages of Palestine in
the First Century A.D.," *CBQ* 32 (1970) 501-31. J. Barr, "Which

Language did Jesus Speak?--Some Remarks of a Semitist," *BJRL* 53
(1971) 9-29. L. Díez Merino, "Es posible hoy reconstruir la
lengua hablada por Jesucristo?" *CuBíb* 29 (1972) 323-30 = *Tierra
Santa* 47 (1972) 307-13. J. A. Emerton, "The Problem of Vernacular
Hebrew in the First Century A. D. and the Language of Jesus,"
JTS 24 (1973) 1-23. M. Delcor, "Le Targum de Job et l'araméen du
temps de Jésus," *RevScRel* 47 (1973) 232-61 = *Exégèse biblique et
Judaïsme* (ed. J. E. Ménard; Leiden: Brill, 1973) 232-61. J.
Fitzmyer, "Some Observations on the Targum of Job from Qumran Cave
11," *CBQ* 36 (1974) 503-24; "The Contribution of Qumran Aramaic to
the Study of the New Testament," *NTS* 20 (1974) 382-407; "Methodology
in the Study of the Aramaic Substratum of Jesus' Sayings in the New
Testament," *Jésus aux origines de la Christologie* (ed. J. Dupont;
BETL 40; Gembloux: Duculot/Louvain University Press, 1975) 73-102.
P. Lapide, "Insights from Qumran into the Languages of Jesus,"
RQ 8 (1972-75) 483-501.

[26]The study of Semitisms and especially Aramaisms in the New
Testament is strictly speaking distinct from the influence of
targumic traditions on NT interpretation, although there is inevit-
ably some overlap, and the Targums are used for examples of Aramaic
constructions and vocabulary. Cf. P. Joüon, *L'Evangile de Notre-
Seigneur Jésus Christ* (Verbum Salutis 5; Paris: Beauchesne, 1930).
A. Wensinck, "Un groupe d'aramäismes dans le texte grec des
Evangiles," *Mededeelingen der koninklijke Akademie van Wetenschappen,
Afdeeling Letterkunde* (Deel 81, Serie A, No. 5; Amsterdam: Uitgevers-
Maatschappij, 1936) 169-80; "The Semitisms of Codex Bezae and their
Relation to the non-Western Text of the Gospel of Saint Luke,"
Bulletin of the Bezan Club 12 (1937) 11-48. C. Torrey, *Our
Translated Gospels* (New York: Harper & Bros., 1938). J. de Zwaan,
"John Wrote in Aramaic," *JBL* 57 (1938) 155-71. A. Olmstead,
"Could an Aramaic Gospel be Written?" *JNES* 1 (1942) 315-40. S.
Feigin, "The Original Language of the Gospels," *JNES* 2 (1943)
187-97. D. Daube, "Concerning the Reconstruction of 'the Aramaic
Gospels'," *BJRL* 29 (1946) 69-105. M. Black, *An Aramaic Approach
to the Gospels and Acts* (Oxford: University Press, 1946; 2nd ed.
1954; 3rd ed. 1967). M. Wilcox, *The Semitisms of Acts* (Oxford:
Clarendon, 1965). R. Le Déaut, "Le substrat araméen des évangiles:
scolies en marge de l'Aramaic Approach de Matthew Black," *Bib*
49 (1968) 388-99.

[27]Cf. "Le Targum palestinien," *RevScRel* 47 (1973) 169-231 =
Exégèse biblique et Judaïsme (ed. J. E. Ménard; Leiden: Brill,
1973) 15-77. *El Targum. Introducción a las traducciones
aramaicas de la Biblia* (Barcelona: CSIC, 1972).

[28]The contents of this chapter may also be found in M. McNamara,
"Targumic Studies," *CBQ* 28 (1966) 1-19.

[29]"Parallelomania," *JBL* 81 (1962) 1-13.

[30]Little or no use of the Targums is made in the following studies.
G.F. Moore, *Judaism* 3 vols. (Cambridge: Harvard University Press,
1927; 10th printing 1966). J. Bonsirven, *Le Judaïsme palestinien
au temps de Jésus-Christ* 2 vols. (Paris: Beauchesne, 1934-35);
Exégèse rabbinique et exégèse paulinienne (Paris: Beauchesne, 1939);
"Judaïsme palestinien au temps de Jésus-Christ," *DBSup* IV 1143-
1285 (Paris: Letouzey et Ané, 1949). English translation *Pales-
tinian Judaism in the Time of Jesus Christ* (New York: Holt,
Rinehart & Winston, 1964). M. Smith, *Tannaitic Parallels to the
Gospels* (SBLMS 6; Philadelphia: SBL, 1951). D. Daube, *The New
Testament and Rabbinic Judaism* (Jordan Lectures 1952; London:
Athlone, 1956). W. D. Davies, *Paul and Rabbinic Judaism* (London:

SPCK, 1948; 2nd ed. 1958; 3rd ed. New York/Evanston: Harper & Row, 1967). Cf. G. Stemberger,"La recherche rabbinique depuis Strack," *RHPR* 55 (1975) 543-74, although the Targums are excluded from this review. The latest study, E. P. Sanders, *Paul and Palestinian Judaism* (London: SCM, 1977), explicitly excludes the use of the Targums on the grounds that the present texts are late. Although he concedes that they contain ancient traditions, he feels the results of contemporary study are not certain enough to serve as a basis for his study.

1. Black, M. "Does an Aramaic Tradition Underlie John 1,16?" *JTS*
42 (1941
The possibility of a word-play on *ḥsd'*, meaning "grace" or
"disgrace"; cf. Frg. Lev 20:17.

2. Black, M. "The Problem of the Aramaic Element in the Gospels,"
ExpTim 59 (1948) 171-76.
B. discusses the revision of Dalman's position regarding Palestinian
Aramaic and the influence of the Tgs. in the Gospels.

3. Black, M. "The Cup Metaphor in Mk. 14,36," *ExpTim* 59 (1948) 195.
Recourse to the OT is not sufficient to explain the metaphor. See
Frg. Gen 40:23: "...the flesh that tasted the cup of death"; cf.
Mark 10:39.

4. Blank, S. H. "The Death of Zachariah in Rabbinic Literature,"
HUCA 12-13 (1937-38) 327-46.
The development of the rabbinic legend that appears in Matt 23:35
and Tg. Lam 2:20 concerning Zachariah, the son of Iddo, high priest
and prophet, killed in the sanctuary.

5. Bloch, R. "Ecriture et tradition dans le judaïsme. Apercus sur
l'origine du midrash," *Cahiers Sioniens* 8 (1954) 9-34.
Midrash has its origins in the interpretation and actualization of
the written Torah. The LXX, Tgs., and NT should be studied in
this light.

6. Bloch, R., "Quelques aspects de la figure de Moïse dans la
tradition rabbinique," *Cahiers Sioniens* 8 (1954) 211-85 = *Moïse,*
l'homme de l'alliance (Paris: Desclée et Cie, 1955) 93-167.
Haggadic traditions about Moses from the Tgs. and the oldest
midrashim. Significance for Matt 1--2; Acts 7; 2 Tim 3:8; the
notions of redemption, new exodus, and a new Moses.

7. Bloch, R. "Note méthodologique pour l'étude de la littérature
rabbinique," *RSR* 43 (1955) 194-227.
A proposed methodology for determining the date of haggadic traditions, especially for use in early Jewish and NT studies. External
criteria are early Jewish works which can be dated; internal

criteria are the developments of a tradition from the OT to Rashi.
Illustrated from traditions concerning the birth of Moses.

8. Bonsirven, J. *Le Judaïsme palestinien au temps de Jésus-Christ*
2 vols. (Paris: Beauchesne, 1934-35).
B. exercises a prudent reserve in the use of the Tgs., while
admitting the presence of ancient traditions in Ps.-J. and Frg. A
targum index (II 491-92) details their use. The expression "second
death" occurs only in Onq., Frg. Deut 33:6 (I 534; cf. Rev 20:6).

9. Bonsirven, J. *Exégèse rabbinique et exégèse paulinienne* (Paris:
Beauchesne, 1939).
Tannaitic sources are used and the Tgs. are explicitly excluded
because of their late date. Nonetheless, Bonsirven does recognize
them as examples of direct exegesis and in some cases acknowledges
that they contain ancient tradition. They are used in a sporadic
manner.

10. Bonsirven, J. "'Hoc est corpus meum.' Recherches sur l'original
araméen," *Bib* 29 (1948) 205-19.
B. opts for *bsr* as the original Aramaic of Jesus. Targumic usage
is discussed, esp. the rendering of *bśr* in Onq. and Ps.-J. Lev;
Num, but is not decisive for B.

11. Bonsirven, J. *Palestinian Judaism in the Time of Jesus Christ*
(New York: Holt, Rinehart & Winston, 1964) = ET of "Judaïsme
palestinien au temps de Jésus-Christ," *DBSup* IV 1143-1285 (Paris:
Letouzey & Ané, 1949).
The same reserve as above; cf. 8.

12. Bowman, J. "The Background of the Term 'Son of Man'," *ExpTim*
59 (1948) 283-88.
A discussion of the targumic rendering of the expression in Pss 8:4;
80:15-17; Ezek; Dan 7:13 and its messianic understanding in Judaism;
Ps.-J. Num 23:19; generic use in CTg. Gen 4:14; 9:5-6. In some
quarters, *bar nash* was a messianic title.

13. Brierre-Narbonne, J. *Exégèse targumique des prophéties
messianiques* (Paris: Geuthner, 1935).
OT messianic texts are reproduced in Hebrew and French with
targumic renderings in Aramaic and French on the facing page.

14. Daube, D. "Concerning the Reconstruction of 'the Aramaic
Gospels'," *BJRL* 29 (1946) 69-105.

The language of the Tgs. is used to offer reservations with respect
to Torrey's theories of mistranslation; e.g. Mark 10:6; Matt 26:64;
Matt 5:48 (cf. Luke 6:36).

15. Davies, W. D. *Torah in the Messianic Age and/or the Age to Come*
(SBLMS 7; Philadelphia: Society of Biblical Literature, 1952).
With respect to the "new teaching" mentioned in Mark 1:27, see Tg.
Isa 12:3;   2:3; 32:6; Cant 5:10 (pp. 70-73).

16. Doeve, J. W. "Le rôle de la tradition orale dans la composition
des évangiles synoptiques," *La Formation des Evangiles* (RechBib 2;
Bruges: Desclée de Brouwer, 1957) 70-84.
Some synoptic variants can only be explained on the basis of an
underlying Aramaic; cf. Mark 9:2 and Luke 9:29 with CTg. Gen 4:5;
also *kai egeneto (kai ginetai)* and CTg. Gen 4:16; 15:11; Lev 1:1.

17. Gärtner, B. "*ṭly'* als Messiasbezeichnung," SEÅ 18-19 (1953-54)
98-108.
A messianic association of *ṭly'*, *'bd*, and *'bn* can be established
on the basis of Tg. Ps 118:22-29--the rejection and sacrifice of
a Messiah-figure; cf. Tg. Zech 3:8-9 for the association of *'bd* and
'bn. This interpretation could hardly be post-Christian; cf. John
1:29, 36; Acts 4:10-12; Matt 21:33-46 (Mark 12:1-12; Luke 20:9-19);
Phil 2:7; 1 Pet 2:4-8; Rom 9:32-33.

18. Hamp, V. *Der Begriff "Wort" in den aramäischen Bibelübersetzungen.*
Ein exegetischer Beitrag zur Hypostasen-Frage und zur Geschichte der
Logos-Spekulation (München: Filser, 1938).
A detailed examination of targumic usage. H. acknowledges a basic
uniformity in the use of the formula *Memra d^e Yahweh*, but also
recognizes significant differences among the Tgs. He sees the
formula primarily as a stylistic and explanatory expression, developing in the later Tgs. practically as a pronoun. He rejects any
special association of the formula with the divine command, or with
creation, and denies any suggestion of an hypostasis in the Tgs.
As such, the formula has practically nothing to do with the prologue
of John or with Christianity.

19. Hegermann, H. *Jesaja 53 in Hexapla, Targum and Peschitta* (BFCT
2, 5-6; Gütersloh: Bertelsmann, 1954).
A comparison of these versions shows that there was a pre-Christian
interpretation of Isa 53 which understood the text in terms of a
suffering Messiah. A relatively late reworking of the Tg. interpreted the suffering of Israel and presented a picture of a

victorious Messiah. The earlier version is reflected in many NT
texts and the preaching of John the Baptist.

20. Joüon, P. *L'Evangile de Notre-Seigneur Jésus Christ* (Verbum
Salutis 5; Paris: Beauchesne, 1930).
A translation of the four Gospels with extensive notes, primarily
of a philological nature dealing with the semitic background of
NT language. The Tgs. are used with respect to Matt 11:26
(Luke 16:24); 18:14; 27:46; Mark 9:43; 15:34; Luke 13:27 (Matt
7:23); 18:14: John 1:1; 4:35.

21. Joüon, P. "Mots grecs de l'araméen d'Onkelos ou de l'hébreu
de la Mishnah qui se trouvent aussi dans les évangiles," *RSR* 22
(1932) 463-69.
Lists of Greek words in transcription found in Onq. and the Mishna.

22. Kahle, P. "Das zur Zeit Jesu in Palästina gesprochene Aramäisch,"
TRu 17 (1949) 201-16 (=*Opera Minora*, Leiden: Brill, 1956, pp. 79-95).
The anti-mishnaic reading of Tg. Exod 22:4-5 indicates the pre-
mishnaic character of the Pal. Tg. as represented by the Cairo
Geniza fragments. K. also notes the appearance of *rabbuni* in these
fragments; cf. Mark 10:51; John 20:16.

23. Kilpatrick, G. D. *The Origin of the Gospel According to St.
Matthew* (Oxford: Clarendon, 1946).
K. recognizes the contacts between Matt 2, the Tgs. and the
Midrashim. He also anticipates R. Bloch's methodology for dating
traditions in the later Tgs. and rabbinic literature.

24. Manson, T.W. "The Old Testament in the Teaching of Jesus,"
BJRL 34 (1952) 312-32.
An examination of the conformity of OT citations with the MT, LXX,
Tgs., or other sources in the Gospels, esp. in the sayings of
Jesus. Jesus quoted the OT from the Hebrew or the Tgs.

25. Michl, J. "Der Weibesame (Gn 3,15) in spätjudischer und
frühchristlicher Auffassung," *Bib* 33 (1952) 371-401; 476-505.
Tg. Gen 3:15 offer a collective understanding of "seed" in contrast
to the LXX and later rabbinic literature. Ps.-J. offers the
possibility of healing in the days of the Messiah, but the latter
is distinguished from the seed of the woman. The collective sense
is reflected in Rom 16:20 and Rev 12.

26. Middleton, R. "Logos and Shekina in the Fourth Gospel," *JQR* 29
(1933) 101-33.

The article deals with the influence of Philo and the Tgs. on the
Fourth Gospel. Special attention is given to the use of Memra,
Shekina, and Yekara in the Tgs. and the appearance of these concepts
in the prologue and throughout the gospel.

27. Plooij, D.   "The Baptism of Jesus," *Amicitiae Corolla*
(Festschrift J. R. Harris; ed. H. G. Wood; London: University
Press, 1933) 239-52.
The voice from heaven is expressed in the language of Jesus'
Bible, i.e. Aramaic. Tg. Ps. 2:7; 80:16; 42:1; 43:10 are discussed
with reference to the NT text.

28. Riesenfeld, H. *Jésus Transfiguré. L'arrière-plan du récit
évangélique de la Transfiguration de notre-Seigneur* (Copenhagen:
Munksgaard, 1947).
The Tgs. are used sporadically to illustrate themes associated with
the Jewish feast of Tabernacles. There is no Targum index.

29. Schoeps, H. J. "The Sacrifice of Isaac in Paul's Theology,"
JBL 65 (1946) 385-92.
Although S. cites Onq. Gen 22:8-9, Jewish literature other than
the Tgs. is used in this article.

30. Seidelin, P. "Der 'Ebed Yahve und die Messiasgestalt im
Jesajatargum," *ZNW* 35 (1936) 194-231.
A study of the targumic rendering of the Servant Songs and other
messianic texts in Isaiah. The targumic picture corresponds to a
late Jewish pre-Christian portrayal of the Messiah. *'bdy* is
associated with the Messiah by way of Tg. Zech 3:8.

31. Sjöberg, E. "Widergeburt und Neuschöpfung im palästinischen
Judentum," *ST* 4 (1951) 44-85.
Some use is made of the Tgs. in connection with the renewal of the
world to come. The Tgs. avoid the idea of God as father and of
Israel as sons of God, but attest the notion of birth from God.

32. Smith, M. "Mt. 5.43: 'Hate Thine Enemy'," *HTR* 45 (1952) 71-73.
The text reflects an Essene oath or a targumic gloss heard in the
synagogues. Ps.-J. Lev 19:18 is glossed differently.

33. Smits, C. *Oud-Testamentische citaten in het Nieuwe Testament*
4 vols. with French summaries (Collectanea Franciscana Neerlandica
VIII 1-4; 's-Hertogenbosch: Malmberg, 1952-63).

These studies do not make explicit use of Tgs., but in some cases
allow for a knowledge of Jewish traditions and freer renderings of
OT texts used in the synagogues.

34. Stendahl, K. *The School of Matthew and Its Use of the Old
Testament* (ASNU 20; Uppsala: Almqvist u. Wiksells, 1954; 2nd ed.
1968).
The liturgical role of the Tgs. is recognized. They may also
contain old Palestinian material. The Tg. of the Prophets is
especially important for the study of Matt's use of the OT. S.
adopts a targumic interpretation where it differs from the OT
and agrees with the NT.

35. Torrey, C. "When I am lifted up from the earth," *JBL* 51 (1932)
320-22.
Hypsothēnai in John 3:14; 8:28; and esp. 12:32-34 renders 'Ithpa^{c}al
of *slq* with the double meaning of "to ascend" and "to depart"; in
the latter sense, cf. Onq. Gen 12:8; 26:22; John 7:33-35.

36. Vermès, G. "La figure de Moïse au tournant des deux Testaments,"
Cahiers Sioniens 8 (1954) 181-210 = *Moïse, l'homme de l'alliance*
(Paris: Desclée et Cie, 1955) 63-92.
The Tgs. are cited several times in this article. Hellenistic
traditions differ from the Palestinian only in their apologetic
aspect and presentation of Moses as a divinely inspired legislator
and wise man.

37. Vermés, G. "Deux traditions sur Balaam--Nombres XXII 2-21 et
ses interprétations midrashiques," *Cahiers Sioniens* 9 (1955)
289-302.
This article appears as the first part of "The Story of Balaam,"
in *Scripture and Tradition in Judaism* (2nd ed. 1973) 127-77.

38. Vermès, G. "A propos des commentaires bibliques découverts à
Qumrân," *RHPR* 35 (1955) 95-103. Also in *La Bible et l'Orient*.
Travaux du premier Congrès d'Archéologie et d'Orientalisme bibliques.
Saint-Cloud 23-25 avril, 1954 (Paris: Presses Universitaires de
France, 1955) 95-103.
The Qumran *pešer* is similar in genre to the Tgs. Neither a midrash
nor a medieval commentary. They approach the revealed exegesis
of the NT.

39. Wikgren, A. "The Targums and the New Testament," *JR* 24 (1944
89-95.

W. encourages recourse to the Tgs. in preference to Torrey's
theories of mistranslation. With Black he suggests that at least
an oral targumic tradition existed in pre-Christian times. The
article anticipates later work concerning targumic traditions and
the NT.

40. Winter, P. "Lc 2,49 and Targum Yerushalmi," *ZNW* 45 (1954)
145-79.
Frg. Exod 15:2 preserves a text in which children admonish their
parents with the words, "God is my father." Jesus could be
presented in Luke 2:41-51a as a teacher of the Law and 2:49 would
simply be a remark of respectful deference.

41. Winter, P. "Lc 2,49 and Targum Yerushalmi again," *ZNW* 46 (1955)
140-41.
Minor corrections to the above article.

42. Winter, P. "Jewish Folklore in the Matthaean Birth Story,"
HibJ 53 (1955) 34-42.
Pharaoh's dream in Ps.-J. Exod 1:15-22 and other non-targumic
material. Cf. also 2 Tim 3:8.

43. Winter, P. "The Cultural Background of the Narrative in Luke I
and II," *JQR* 45 (1955) 159-67; 230-42.
The author of Luke 1--2 was familiar with Palestinian culture and
tradition, even though other passages indicate otherwise. The
following texts are discussed with some targumic references:
1:5, 9, 9-10, 19, 58; 2:8, 37.

44. Winter, P. "Some Observations on the Language in the Birth-
and Infancy- Stories of the Third Gospel," *NTS* 1 (1955) 111-21.
Reference is made to the messianism of Luke 2:4-18 in connection
with Ps.-J. Gen 35:21 (p.116).

PART II   SINCE 1956

80. Aalen, S. "'Reign' and 'House' in the Kingdom of God in the Gospels," *NTS* 8 (1962) 215-40.
The Nathan prophecy in 2 Sam 7 and 1 Chr 17 and Tgs. 1 Chr 17:14 and Tg. may be the source for the local sense of the kingdom of God; associated with the notion of the royal "house" as a community (Tg. 2 Sam 7:11; 1 Sam 2:35; 1 Chr 17:10). "House" of John 8:35; 14:2 is identical with the kingdom of God in John 3:3, 5. Application to other NT texts also indicated.

81. Aalen, S. "Das Abendmahl als Opfermahl im Neuen Testament," *Charis kai Sophia* (Festschrift K. H. Rengstorf; Leiden: Brill, 1964) 128-52.
The targumists exclude the sprinkling of the people with blood and the sacrificial meal from the establishment of the convenant; cf. Onq., Ps.-J. Exod 24:8; Onq., Frg., Ps.-J., Neof. Exod 24:11b. The NT eucharistic texts associate them. In the Eucharist, as covenant sacrificial meal, we do not share a meal with God but share in the sacrificial event.

82. Aberbach, M., Grossfeld, B. *Targum Onqelos on Genesis 49. Translation and Commentary* (SBL Aramaic Studies 1; Missoula: Scholars Press ,1976).
Messianic interpretations of Gen 49 and Zech 9:9 are indicated in the notes, with a few NT references.

83. Aufrecht, W. E. (editor) *Newsletter for Targumic and Cognate Studies* (Toronto: Victoria College, 1974-).
Information concerning congresses, work done, and work in progress. Appears intermittently each year.

84. Barr, J. "Which Language did Jesus Speak?--Some Remarks of a Semitist," *BJRL* 53 (1971) 9-29.
Aramaic Tgs. did not necessarily supply for the ignorance of Hebrew, but served as a paraphrastic interpretation of the written Scriptures.

85. Barrett, C. K. "Luke 22, 15: To Eat the Passover," *JTS* 9 (1958) 305-07.
The expression *phagein to pascha* may mean "to eat this lamb" and not refer to the whole passover ritual. Cf. MT, LXX, and Tg.

25

Exod 12:11; 12:43-46; Num 9:10-11; Deut 16:2-3; 16:7; 2 Chr 30:18;
Ezra 6:20-21.

86. Bartina, S. "Aportaciones recientes de los targumim a la
interpretación neotestamentaria," *EstE* 39 (1964) 361-76.
Twenty-seven examples of light thrown on NT texts by the Pal. Tgs.

87. Baumstark, A. "Die Zitate des Mt.-Evangeliums aus dem
Zwölfprophetenbuch," *Bib* 37 (1956) 296-313.
A discussion of the targumizing character of Matthew's citations
from the minor prophets, with support from the Samaritan Pentateuch
and the Pal. Tgs. The Aramaic Matthew may have used a targum of
the Twelve.

88. Bernhardt, K. "Zu Eigenart und Alter der messianisch-eschatologischen Zusätze im Targum Jeruschalmi I," *Gott und die Götter*
(Festschrift E. Fascher; Berlin: Evangelische Verlagsanstalt,
1958) 68-83.
B. dates this material to the 10th-11th cent. A. D.

89. Betz, O. "Zungenreden und süsser Wein. Zur eschatologischen
Exegese von Jesaja 28 in Qumran and im Neuen Testament," *Bibel
und Qumran. Beiträge zur Erforschung der Beziehungen zwischen
Bibel- und Qumranwissenschaft* (Festschrift H. Bardtke; Berlin:
Evangelische Haupt-Bibelgesellschaft, 1968) 20-36.
Qumran, the Tg., and the LXX understand Isa 28:7-13 of the
intelligible language of pagans. 1 Cor 14:21 and Acts 2 apply
the text to glossolalia as a prophetic sign (cf. Acts 19:6). The
rabbinic understanding of the Sinai tradition serves as a background
for the language miracle of Pentecost.

90. Black, M. "Die Erforschung der Muttersprache Jesu," *TLZ* 82
(1957) 653-68.
The article concerns sources for Palestinian Aramaic at the time
of Jesus. The value of the Pal. Tgs. is discussed (pp. 660-64)
with respect to Dalman's earlier position, and the importance of
1QapGen (pp. 664-68). Cf. Acts 7:2 and Gen 14:1 in 1QapGen 22:27
and Tgs. (p. 666).

91. Black, M. "The Recovery of the Language of Jesus," *NTS* 3 (1957)
305-13.
The importance of the Pal. Tgs. for the knowledge of 1st cent.
Aramaic. A first report on Neofiti 1 and 1QapGen; cf. Acts 7:2
and 1QapGen 22:27.

92. Black, M. *An Aramaic Approach to the Gospels and Acts* (Oxford:
University Press, 1946; 2nd ed. 1954; 3rd ed. 1967).
Unpublished material of A. J. Wensinck in the 2nd ed. Chap. 3 of
Part I, dealing with Qumran and Neofiti added to the 3rd ed.; also
an Appendix by G. Vermès, "The Use of BAR NASH/BAR NASHA in Jewish
Aramaic." The study contains a review of scholarship concerning
Aramaisms and Aramaic sources. Black prefers the indirect influ-
ence of Aramaic sources on the targumizing of Greek writers of
Semitic origin. Tgs. are frequently cited as evidence. No Targum
index.

93. Black, M. "The 'Son of Man' Passion Sayings in the Gospel
Tradition," *ZNW* 60 (1969) 1-8.
The role of Isa, Dan, Hos, Pss, Tg. Isa 53:12; Hos 6:1-2 and the
ambiguous *zdgyp* in the formation of the passion sayings, esp.
Rom 4:25; 1 Cor 15:4; John 3:14.

94. Black, M. "Ephphatha (Mk 7.34), Ta Pascha (Mt 26.18W), Ta
Sabbata (passim), [Ta] Didrachma (Mt 17.24 bis)," *Mélanges
bibliques en hommage au R. P. Béda Rigaux* (edd. A. Descamps, A. de
Halleux; Gembloux: Duculot, 1970) 57-62.
Neof. m. Gen 3:7 offers another example of an assimilated *t* in
'Ithpa^cal of *pth*. Vs. Rabinowitz, *ephphatha* could be Aramaic.

95. Black, M. "The Christological Use of the Old Testament in the
New Testament," *NTS* 18 (1972) 1-14.
Evidence from the OT, Qumran, and the Tgs. concerning pre-Christian
traditions of messianic import concerning the titles *Christos,
Kyrios, huios theou,* and *ho huios tou anthrōpou.* Esp. Tg. Hos 6:2;
Ps 118:22.

96. Bloch, R. "'Juda engendra Pharès et Zara de Thamar' (Matth. 1,3),"
Mélanges bibliques rédigés en l'honneur d'André Robert (Paris:
Bloud & Gay, 1957) 381-89.
Jewish traditions concerning Tamar and Judah beginning with Frg.
Gen 38: 25-26 and Ps.-J. Gen 38:1-30. Role of providence and of
Tamar as an ancestress of the Messiah.

97. Boismard, M.-E. *Du Baptême à Cana* (LD 18; Paris: Cerf, 1956).
On pp. 123-27, Ps.-J. Gen 28:12-13 is used to explain John 1:51.

98. Boismard, M.-E. "De son ventre couleront des fleuves d'eau
(Jo., VII, 38)," *RB* 65 (1958) 523-46.
Ek tēs koilias autou derives from an original Aramaic phrase *mn*

gwh ("from within him"). Tg. Ps 78:16 may explain the rest of
the citation.

99. Boismard, M.-E. "Les citations targumiques dans le quatrième
évangile," *RB* 66 (1959) 374-78.
B. defends his translation of Tg. Ps 78:16 against Grelot's
criticism; cf. 191. Suggests also the influence of Pal. Tg. Deut
18:18-19 on John 12:48-49, and of Pal. Tg. Num 21:8-9 on John
3:14-15, 18.

99a. Boismard, M.-E., Lamouille, A. *Synopse des quatre évangiles
en francais.* Tome III. *L'évangile de Jean* (Paris: Cerf, 1977).
Use of Tgs. is indicated in the Alphabetic Index (p. 559).

100. Bonneau, N. R. "The Woman at the Well. John 4 and Genesis
24," *IBT* no. 67 (1973) 1252-59.
Gen 24 and Exod 2 as synagogue readings and literary background
for John 4. Pal. Tg. Num 21:16-18 and Gen 29 concerning the
welling up of water and the role of Jacob.

101. Boobyer, G. "The Verbs in Jude 11," *NTS* 5 (1959) 45-47.
In the light of Jewish tradition, including the Pal. Tgs., all
three verbs indicate punishment and death.

102. Borgen, P. "Observations on the Targumic Character of the
Prologue of John," *NTS* 16 (1970) 288-95.
John 1:1-5 is a midrashic exposition of Gen 1:1-5 (abc), and John
1:6-18 an elaboration in reverse order (cba), applying the text
of Genesis to the Logos and Jesus respectively. The same manner
of treating Gen 1:1-5 is found in the Pal. Tg. Gen 3:24.

103. Bowker, J. "Speeches in Acts: A Study in Proem and Yelammedenu
Form," *NTS* 14 (1968) 96-111.
The "proem" form of the Jewish synagogue homily may be seen in
Acts 13:16-41; 2:21-39; 3:12-26; 7:2-53. The "yelammedenu" form
may be seen in Acts 15:14-21; Rom 4; 3:10-20; 9:6--11:10; Gal 3:6-
14: the solution of a halakic question by reference to past exper-
ience and to Scripture. Some use of Tgs., esp. 1 Sam 13:14;
Gen 15:6.

104. Bowker, J. *The Targums and Rabbinic Literature. An Introduction
to Jewish Interpretations of Scripture* (Cambridge: University Press,
1969).
A general introduction to the Tgs., pre-rabbinic, non-rabbinic, and
classical rabbinic literature. Contains an English translation

of selected chaps. of Ps.-J. Gen with comments from other Tgs. and Jewish traditions.

105. Bowker, J. "The Son of Man," *JTS* 28 (1977) 19-48.
A criticism of Vermès position on *bar nash(a)* as a circumlocution for "I." Usage in OT and Tgs. contrasts human weakness and subjection to death with the majesty of God and of the angels. This usage, combined with divine vindication of the Son of Man in Dan 7, could be authentic in Mark and in continuity with Chalcedonian Christianity.

106. Bowman, J. *The Gospel of Mark. The New Christian Jewish Passover Haggadah* (SPB 8: Leiden: Brill, 1965).
Messianic texts of the OT were familiar to the people through the activity of the *meturgeman*. Ch. 6 (pp. 65-74) deals with Tg. Isa 53 and the Messiah. A Targum entry in the subject index indicates other references, esp. in relation to Mark 13:14-25 (pp. 246-47).

107. Brown, R. E. *The Gospel according to John* (AB 29; 29A; New York: Doubleday, 1966-70).
B. acknowledges the possibility that John is citing from the Pal. Tg. in several places and referring to it elsewhere; e.g. 3:14; 4:6; 4:12; 4:20; 7:38; 12:41; 12:47-48; 20:23. The Tgs. are also referred to with reference to the Memra and the prologue; cf. also 3:18.

108. Burchard, C. "Das Lamm in der Waagschale. Herkunft und Hintergrund eines haggadischen Midraschs zu Ex 1, 15-22," *ZNW* 57 (1966) 219-28.
A rejection of K. Koch's thesis. The haggadic legend of Pharaoh's dream has its origin in medieval midrashim; Ps.-J. Exod 1:15 is independent and later. Koch's use of the demotic papyrus is not to the point.

109. Cantinat, J. *Les Epîtres de Saint Jacques et de Saint Jude* (SB; Paris: Gabalda, 1973).
Jude 11 and Ps.-J. Gen 4:7; Neof. Num 22:30 concerning Cain and Balaam respectively (p. 312).

110. Cave, C. H. "The Parables and the Scriptures," *NTS* 11 (1965) 374-87.
Tg. Jer 4:3; Hos 10:21; Ezek 17:22-24 are used by the author in an attempt to recover the sermon setting for the parable of the sower, the seed growing secretly, and the mustard seed. Cf. also Matt 3:8.

111. Clarke, E. G. "Jacob's Dream as Interpreted in the Targums and
the New Testament," *SR* 4 (1975) 367-77.
The Pal. Tg. traditions contained in Gen 28:10-22 predate Onqelos
and have influenced the presentation of Jesus in John 4:7-15,
20-24; 1:51.   "The New Testament parallels indicate the antiquity
of the targumic traditions."

112. Cortès, E. *Los discorsos de adiós de Gn 49 a Jn 13--17. Pistas
para la historia de un género literario en la antigua literatura
judía* (Colectánea San Paciano XXIII; Barcelona: Editorial Herder,
1976).
Farewell discourses in the OT, the Tgs., intertestamental literature
are studied as a background for John 13--17.   The Tgs. of Gen 49
and Deut 33 include an exhortation to purification by profession of
faith, fraternal union, works of mercy, and conclude with a
testament.   Prophecies become more detailed, messianic and
eschatological doctrine is explicitated, and the theme of revelation
appears.   Concerning purification, cf. John 13:10; 15:3 and the
concept of *pswl*.

113. Cowling, G. J.   "New Light on the New Testament?   The
Significance of the Palestinian Targum," *Theological Students'
Fellowship Bulletin* 51 (1968) 6-14.

114. Cowling, G. J. "Targum Neofiti, Exodus 16:15," *AJBA* (1975)
93-105.
Vermès' reading of Neof. Exod 16:15, "He is the bread," is based
on a scribal error.   Ps.-J. is a late revision of Onq. with
Palestinian tendencies.   Neof. should be dated after the 3rd or
4th cent. A. D. on linguistic grounds.

115. Dahl, N. A. "Der Erstgeborene Satans und der Vater des Teufels
(Polyk. 7.1 und Joh 8.44), *Apophoreta* (Festschrift E. Haenchen;
BZNW 30; Berlin: Töpelmann, 1964) 70-84.
Targumic and midrashic traditions concerning Cain as the offspring
of Satan and the first heretic pre-date Polycarp and are reflected
in John 8:44 (present text defective) and 1 John 3:12, 15.   Cf.
2 Cor 11:14; 11:2-3; 1 Tim 2:14-15; also Pal. Tg. Gen 4:8 and
John 8:59; 10:31; 11:8--Cain killed Abel with a stone!

116. Dahl, N. A. "The Atonement--An Adequate Reward for the Akedah?
(Ro 8:32)," *Neotestamentica et Semitica* (Festschrift M. Black;
Edinburgh: T. & T. Clark, 1969) 15-29.
A pre-Pauline Jewish-Christian midrash already saw the atoning

death of Christ as God's merciful response to Abraham's prayer at
the time of the sacrifice of Isaac. Other NT texts are discussed
in the light of the Akedah tradition.

117. Dahl, N. A. "'A People for His Name' (Acts xv.14)," *NTS* 4
(1958) 319-27.
The formula is not found in the LXX, but is a standard idiom of
the Pal. Tg. It does not correspond with *segullâ*.

118. Daly, R. J. "The Soteriological Significance of the Sacrifice
of Isaac," *CBQ* 39 (1977) 45-75.
A review of scholarly opinions concerning the influence of the
Akedah tradition on NT soteriology, esp. Paul. It is possible
that the Pal. Tgs. exercised a direct influence on NT thought.
NT references to Isaac are classified as certain, probable, and
possible.

119. Daube, D. *The New Testament and Rabbinic Judaism* (Jordan
Lectures 1952; London: Athlone, 1956).
Methods of rabbinic exegesis reflected in NT texts. Rabbinic
literature is predominantly used, with rare references to the Tgs.

120. Daube, D. "The Earliest Structure of the Gospels," *NTS* 5
(1959) 174-87.
The passover haggada was a matrix of the Gospels. Pp. 184-86
discuss the influence of the Laban legend on Matt 2:13-18; Laban
was identified with Balaam (Frg. Num 22:5) and sought to destroy
all infants.

121. Davies, W. D. *Paul and Rabbinic Judaism* (London: SPCK, 1948;
2nd ed. 1955; 3rd ed. New York/Evanston: Harper & Row, 1967).
Ten independent studies with a conclusion. The 3rd ed. is a
reprint of the 2nd, plus a study on "Paul and Judaism" taken from
The Bible in Modern Scholarship (ed. J. P. Hyatt; New York/
Nashville: Abingdon, 1965). The Tgs. play a very small role in
D.'s work, but there is a Targum index.

122. Davies, W. D. *The Setting of the Sermon on the Mount* (Cambridge:
University Press, 1964).
In reaction to Jewish eschatological expectations and to the work
of Jamnia, the "law" of Jesus is not presented as a new Torah.
Some use is made of the Tgs. but rabbinic literature predominates.

123. De Jonge, M. "Jewish Expectations about the 'Messiah' according
to the Fourth Gospel," *NTS* 19 (1973) 246-70.

The messianic interpretation of Tg. Mic 5:1, 3 is mentioned with
reference to Matt 2:5, 6 and John 7:40-44. The Johannine text
reflects Jewish-Christian debate and is no proof of a Jewish
understanding of the Messiah from Bethlehem.

124. Delcor, M. "La portée chronologique de quelques interprétations
du Targoum Néophyti contenues dans le cycle d'Abraham," *JSJ* 1
(1970) 105-19.
Targumic and other Jewish traditions concerning Abraham as the
father of proselytes (cf. Matt 3:9), the oak of Mamre as the plains
of vision, Abraham saved from the fiery furnace, and the angels
who appear to eat. Evidence for dating Neofiti 1 as a whole in
the 1st or 2nd century A. D. with pre-Christian roots.

125. Delcor, M. "Le Targum de Job et l'araméen du temps de Jésus,"
RevScRel 47 (1973) 232-61 = *Exégèse biblique et Judaïsme* (ed.
J.-E. Ménard; Leiden: Brill, 1973) 78-107.
A review of the language problem. Qumran shows the influence of
spoken Aramaic on imperial Aramaic. There are dangers in seeking
the spoken language in the Pal. Tgs. Semantic considerations
must supplement syntactical and morphological considerations.
Joüon now inadequate.

126. Delling, G. "Zum gottesdienstlichen Stil der Johannes-
Apokalypse," *NovT* 3 (1959) 107-37.
The threefold designation of God in Rev 1:4, 8; 4:8 reflects
Jewish exegesis and Pal. Tg. Deut 32:39; Exod 3:14, but D. does not
suggest direct dependence in either direction (pp. 122-27).

127. Derrett, J. D. M. *Law in the New Testament* (London: Darton,
Longman & Todd, 1970).
A revised form of earlier studies plus three new studies. D.
recognizes the importance of the Tgs. for 1st cent. Judaism and,
in dependence on Kahle, makes use of them throughout his study.

128. De Waard, J. "The Quotation from Deuteronomy in Acts 3, 22.23
and the Palestinian Text: Additional Arguments," *Bib* 52 (1971)
537-40.
Acts 3:22-23 as a witness to the Palestinian form of Deut 18:18-19
in the light of *4Q175* and Ps.-J., Onq., and Neof. Possible non-
LXX background for Deut citations in the speeches of Acts.

129. De Zwaan, J. "John Wrote in Aramaic," *JBL* 57 (1938) 155-71.
A discussion of C. Torrey *Our Translated Gospels* (1936). Tg. Ps
46:5-8 and John 7:38 (pp. 165-66).

130. Díaz, J. Ramón.   "Dos notas sobre el Targum palestinense,"
Sef 19 (1959) 133-36.
The relation of CTg. Exod 20:13-17 and Rom 5:12. Cain and justifi-
cation in Tg. Gen 4:8-11; the Cairo text is the older.

131. Díaz, J. Ramón.   "Targum Palestinense y Nuevo Testamento,"
EstBíb 21 (1962) 337-42.
Examples of NT texts illustrated by the Tgs.: John 4:15; 1 Pet 1:12;
Eph 4:22-25 (cf. Col 3:9); "flesh" in Paul (e.g. Rom 8:5, 6);
John 8:39-45; 1 John 3:8-12.

132. Díaz, J. Ramón.   "Palestinian Targum and the New Testament,"
NovT 6 (1963) 75-80.
A short survey of the field of study, with NT illustrations.

133. Díez Macho, A. "Una copia de todo el Targum jerosolimitano
en la Vaticana," *EstBíb* 15 (1956) 446-47.
A first report on the identification of Neofiti 1. An English
translation appeared in *NTS* 3 (1957) 307.

134. Díez Macho, A. "Una copia completa del Targum Palestinense al
Pentateuco en la Bibliotheca vaticana," *Sef* 17 (1957) 119-21.
A first report on the identification of Neofiti 1.

135. Díez Macho, A.   "The Recently Discovered Palestinian Targum:
Its Antiquity and Relationship with the other Targums," VTSup 7
(Leiden: Brill, 1960) 222-45.
The antiquity of the Pal. Tg. in the light of Neofiti 1. D.
argues for an early date for the Pal. Tg. and for a proto-Onqelos.
The article includes examples of NT dependence on the Pal. Tgs.
which have already been proposed.

136. Díez Macho, A.   "La lengua hablada por Jesucristo," *OrAnt* 2
(1963) 95-132.
Evidence, new and old, for the use of Hebrew, Greek, and Aramaic
in 1st cent. Palestine. D. favors the substantial identity of
Galilean and Judean Aramaic.

137. Díez Macho, A. "El Logos y el Espíritu Santo," *Atlándida* 1
(1963) 381-96.
Neofiti 1, esp. Gen 1:1--2:4a, is used as evidence for the use of
Memra in the synagogues of 1st cent. Palestine. Cf. also Neof.
Exod 12:42: the Memra of Yahweh enlightens the darkness of the
cosmos; cf. John 1:1-18. John's use of Logos is directly related
through synagogue usage with the OT tendency to personify God's

Wisdom and Word; this tendency disappears in later rabbinic
literature. "The holy spirit" is used frequently in Neofiti 1
and in Qumran literature; cf. John 14:26; 15:26; 16:13-15.

138. Díez Macho, A. "Targum y Nuevo Testamento," *Mélanges Eugène
Tisserant* I (Studi e Testi 231; Città del Vaticano: Biblioteca
Apostolica Vaticana, 1964) 153-85.
Earlier neglect of the Tgs. has been replaced by new interest due
to the work of P. Kahle and the identification of Neofiti 1.
Fifty examples of the use of Targums in NT interpretation from
recent literature.

139. Díez Macho, A. "El 'targum' en la liturgia de la Iglesia,"
Apostolado Sacerdotal 23 (1967) 33-39.
The role of a "targum"-type translation for the liturgy alongside
a more literal translation.

140. Díez Macho, A. *El Targum. Introducción a las traducciones
aramaicas de la Biblia* (Barcelona: CSIC, 1972).
A general introduction to contemporary Targum study. Their
importance for the knowledge of ancient Jewish tradition, the
exegesis of the NT, and the knowledge of Palestinian Aramaic at
the time of Jesus.

141. Díez Macho, A. "Le targum palestinien," *RevScRel* 47 (1973)
169-231 = *Exégèse biblique et Judaïsme* (ed. J.-E. Ménard; Leiden:
Brill, 1973) 15-77.
A summary of Targum editions to date, studies and problems.
Importance of the Pal. Tgs. for knowledge of early Jewish halaka
and haggada, for the history of exegesis in the OT and the NT,
for the Aramaic substratum of the Gospels and Acts, and for the
textual criticism of the NT. Pp. 201-14 deal, for the most part,
with work already accomplished in the area of Tgs. and NT
interpretation.

142. Díez Macho, A. "Deraš y Exegesis del Nuevo Testamento," *Sef*
35 (1975) 37-89.
Contemporary study of midrashic exegesis and the presence of these
methods in the NT. The contribution of the Tgs. is mentioned in
several places.

143. Díez Macho, A. "Un nuevo manuscrito del Targum fragmentario,"
Homenaje a Juan Prado (edd. L. Alvarez Verdes y E. Alonso Hernandez;
Madrid: CSIC, 1975) 533-51.

On pp. 544-547 D. indicates further evidence from Ms. 6684 of the
Frg. Tg. at the National and University Library of Jerusalem for
the assimilation of *t* in Palestinian Aramaic, thus supporting the
arguments of others for an Aramaic form at Mark 7:34: *ephphatha*.

144. Díez Macho, A. *El Mesías Anunciado y Esperado. Perfil
Humano de Jésus* (Colleción Santiago Apostol; Madrid: Fe Católica,
1976).
The text of two conferences with annotations. The first conference
incorporates the messianic interpretations of the Tgs. The second
conference mentions Pal. Tg. Gen 38:26 and other Jewish sources
with reference to Matt 7:2; Mark 4:24; Luke 6:38.

145. Díez Macho, A. *La historicidad de los Evangelios de la
Infancia. El entorno de Jésus* (Colleción Santiago Apostol; Madrid:
Fe Católica, 1977).
The text of two conferences with annotations. Jewish traditions
as exhibited in the Tgs. and other Jewish traditions are used in
elucidating the infancy gospels. In the second conference, Tg.
Lam is referred to with reference to Luke 4:18.

146. Díez Macho, A. *Resurreción de Jesucristo y de la hombre en la
Biblia* (Colleción Santiago Apostol; Madrid: Fe Católica, 1977).
D. discusses the resurrection in terms of dualistic and monistic
anthropology with reference to the OT, intertestamental literature
and the NT. The Tgs. are used where pertinent.

147. Díez Merino, L. *La vocación de Abraham (Gen 12,1-4a). La
vocación de Abraham en el Antiguo Testamento, Nuevo Testamento y
Tradición Judía Antigua.* Dissertation *Studium Biblicum Franciscanum*
(Jerusalem, 1969).
The published extract (Rome: Pontificio Ateneo Antoniano, 1970)
deals only with the OT. Part II deals with the NT (Gal 3; Rom 4;
John 8:31-59); Part III deals with Jewish tradition including the
Tgs.

148. Díez Merino, L. "Es posible hoy reconstruir la lengua
hablada por Jesu-cristo?" *CuBíb* 29 (1972) 323-30. Also *Tierra
Santa* 47 (1972) 307-13.
Neofiti 1 is a witness to the Galilean Aramaic spoken by Jesus.

149. Díez Merino, L. "Aportación española al VIII Congreso de la
'Organización Internacional para el estudio del Antiguo Testamento'
(Edimburgo 18-23 de agosto 1974)," *EstE* 50 (1975) 129-39.

The article includes a summary of a paper by Díez Merino, "El
Decálogo en el Targum Palestinense." The development of the tradition in Judaism. Its use by the Minim as a summary of the Law
(cf. Mark 10:17, 19) led to its disappearance from the daily
prayers of the Jews.

150. Díez Merino, L. "El Decalogo en el Targum Palestinense. Origen,
Estilo y Motivaciones," *EstBíb* 34 (1975) 23-48.
The article is primarily concerned with the targumic text and the
disappearance of the Decalogue from the daily prayers in later
Judaism; Christian use of the Decalogue as a summary of the Law
may have played some role; cf. Mark 10:17-19 (Matt 19:16-19;
Luke 18:18-20).

151. Díez Merino, L. "La crucifixión en la antigua literature judía
(Periodo intertestamental), *EstE* 51 (1976) 5-27.
The practice of crucifixion in Judaism as a capital punishment,
and the jurisdiction of the Sanhedrin prior to the destruction of
the Temple. The evidence of Tg. Deut 21:22-23; Num 25:4; Lev 19:26;
Ruth 1:17; Esth I 9:14; II 9:12; 7:9 is presented and evaluated.
John 18:31 reflects a Pharisaic position after 70.

152. Díez Merino, L. "El suplicio de la Cruz en la literatura
Judía intertestamental," *SBFLA* 26 (1976) 31-120.
An expanded form of the article which appeared in *EstE* 51 (1976)
5-27; cf. 151.

153. Di Nola, A. "Targumim," *Enciclopedia delle Religioni* (Firenze:
Vallecchi, 1973) V 1645-57.
The major portion of the article is devoted to bibliography.

154. Dip, G. "Plegaria y sufrimento del siervo de Yavé," *EstE* 41
(1966) 303-50.
Tg. Isa 53 is treated on pp. 310-19 (cf. also p. 327). The work
of the Servant-Messiah in Tg. Isa 53 is treated like the priestly
work of expiation in Lev 4:20-35 and Tg., to avoid the concept of
a suffering Messiah. The language of intercession was used in the
revision of Tg. Isa 53, because *kipper* connoted vicarious expiation
in contemporary Judaism.

155. Dupont, J. "L'appel à imiter Dieu en Matthieu 5,48 et Luc 6,36,"
RivB 14 (1966) 137-58.
Pal. Tg. Lev 22:28 confirms the priority of Luke 6:36. In Luke God
is the exemplar of our actions; in Matt God's action in our regard
is based on our actions. Jesus looks to God first.

156. Dupont, J. "'*Laos ex ethnōn*' (Ac 15,14)," *NTS* 3 (1957) 47-50 =
Etudes sur les Actes des Apôtres (LD 45; Paris: Cerf, 1967) 361-65
with an additional note.
In the additional note, D. accepts Dahl's suggestion of a popular
formula based on the Tgs., rather than a specific text. Cf. Tg.
Zech 2:15.

157. Elliott, J. H. *The Elect and the Holy. An Exegetical
Examination of 1 Peter 2:4-10 and the Phrase basileion hierateuma*
(NovTSup 12; Leiden: Brill, 1966).
The priesthood concerned in this text is non-Levitical. The
targumic version of Exod 19:6 is studied on pp. 76-79. The targumic
interpretation of the "stone"-texts, Isa 8:14; 28:16; Ps 118:22,
are treated on pp. 25-28. E. affirms a pre-Christian messianic
interpretation of these "stone"-texts. There is a Targum index.

158. Ellis, E. E. *Paul's Use of the Old Testament* (Grand Rapids:
Eerdmans, 1957).
A comprehensive study of the question to date. E. cautiously
acknowledges the direct use of Tgs. in some cases. "In many cases
the Pauline rendering is intimately connected with his application
of the text. These applications make use of common stock
interpretations, oral and targumic traditions, and rabbinic
methodology" (p. 148). There is no Targum index.

159. Ellis, E. E. "Midrash, Targum and New Testament Quotations,"
Neotestamentica et Semitica (Festschrift M. Black; Edinburgh:
T. & T. Clark, 1969) 61-69.
The importance of understanding OT citations in the NT in the light
of Jewish targumizing and midrash.

160. Ellis, E. E. "Midrashic Features in the Speeches of Acts,"
Mélanges bibliques en hommage au R. P. Béda Rigaux (edd. A.
Descamps et A. de Halleux; Gembloux: Duculot, 1970) 303-12.
Targumic traditions reflected in the use of OT texts. In the NT
the argument generally proceeds from the current events to the
text of Scripture, and not vice versa.

161. Ellis, E. E. "Midraschartige Züge in den Reden der
Apostelgeschichte," *ZNW* 62 (1971) 94-104.
An enlarged form of the article which appeared in the Rigaux
Festschrift. Cf. 160.

162. Emerton, J. A. "Some New Testament Notes," *JTS* 11 (1960)
329-36.

With reference to John 10:34, Tg. Ps 82 understands "gods" in
v. 1 of men, and of angels in v. 6. E. explains the text in terms
of beings to whom God has given authority, viz. angels. Mark
10:45 is not dependent on Isa 53; Aramaic ^{c}bd in 'Ithpe^{c}el cannot
mean "to be served."

163. Emerton, J. A. "Binding and Loosing--Forgiving and Retaining,"
JTS 13 (1962) 325-31.

The article concerns the Aramaic background and tradition history
of Matt 16:19; 18:18; John 20:23. The earliest form of the saying
in Matt 16 followed Isa 22:22. *Pth* and *'hd* of Tg. Isa 22:22
explain *aphienai* and *kratein* of John 20:23; Matt adapted to rabbinic
use of *šr'* (*šbq*) and *'šr* substituted for *'hd*. Matt 16 adapted to
a group in Matt 18 and John 20.

164. Emerton, J. A. "Mark XIV,24 and the Targum to the Psalter,"
JTS 15 (1964) 58-59.

Aramaic evidence from Tg. Pss 68:36; 110:3 added to previous
Syriac evidence for the grammatical possibility of the formula
to haima mou tēs diathēkēs.

165. Faur, J. "The Targumim and Halakha," *JQR* 66 (1976) 19-26.

"The problems that T(argums) of the type of Neofiti I posed to
the Rabbinic authorities are, to my mind, the major reason for
their limited circulation and eventually almost complete
oblivion" (p. 26).

166. Feigin, S. "The Original Language of the Gospels," *JNES* 2
(1943) 187-97.

Against Goodspeed, cf. 185, F. supports the existence of early
written Tgs. and the possibility of Hebrew or Aramaic gospels in
the first century. He affirms the midrashic character of the
gospels and discusses Jewish evidence for Christian literature.
Matt 5:48 (cf. Luke 6:36) is explained as a misreading of Frg.
Lev 22:28 (*tamin* for *rhmin*; p. 196).

167. Feuillet, A. *Le Prologue du Quatrième Evangile. Etude de
théologie johannique* (Paris: Desclée de Brouwer, 1968).

Pp. 244-48 discuss the influence of Philo and the rabbinic
concepts of Torah and Memra on the Johannine Logos. Earlier
positions concerning Memra are compared with recent work.

168. Fitzmyer, J. "'Now this Melchizedek...' (Heb 7:1)," *CBQ* 25
(1963) 205-21 = *Essays on the Semitic Background of the New
Testament* (London: Geoffrey Chapman, 1971) 221-43.
Heb 7 as a midrash on Gen 14:18-20 in the light of 1QapGen and Neof.

169. Fitzmyer, J. "The Languages of Palestine in the First
Century A. D.," *CBQ* 32 (1970) 501-31.
Aramaic the most commonly used language with growing evidence for
the use of Greek and Hebrew. Aramaic documentation is also growing.
Greek influence on Aramaic is only attested from the 2nd cent.
A. D. and later. Greek words in the Tgs. are not evidence of an
early date.

170. Fitzmyer, J. "Some Observations on the Targum of Job from
Qumran Cave 11," *CBQ* 36 (1974) 503-24.
Memra is not used in 11QtgJob 38:2-4 as it is used in Tg. Job
42:9-10. Implications of 11QtgJob for Aramaic of NT times.

171. Fitzmyer, J. "The Contribution of Qumran Aramaic to the Study
of the New Testament," *NTS* 20 (1974) 382-407.
Aramaic texts from Qumran related to the titles of Jesus in the
NT; Jewish practices and beliefs, literary parallels with the NT.
Published texts of Palestinian Aramaic and Qumran Aramaic are
listed.

172. Fitzmyer, J. "Methodology in the Study of the Aramaic Substratum of Jesus' Sayings in the New Testament," *Jésus aux
origines de la Christologie* (ed. J. Dupont; BETL 40; Gembloux:
Duculot/Louvain University Press, 1975) 73-102.
The present state of the question. More evidence is required for
the spoken Aramaic of the 1st cent. A. D. New evidence for
qorban, *'škḥ* = "to be able" (Luke 6:7; 13:24), mistranslation at
Matt 7:6; remarks on the Son of Man. F. admits early literary
traditions in the Tgs.

173. Flusser, D. "Sanktus und Gloria," *Abraham unser Vater*
(Festschrift O. Michel; AGSU 5; Leiden: Brill, 1963) 129-52.
Luke 2:14 is a paraphrase of the Trisagion of Isa 6:3 via the Pal.
Tgs. and Jewish liturgy. Cf. Tg. Ezek 3:12.

174. Flusser, D. "A New Sensitivity in Judaism and the Christian
Message," *HTR* 61 (1968) 107-27.
Ps.-J. Lev 19:18, 34 and Matt 7:12. The problem of altruistic
love in Judaism.

175. Ford, J. M. "'He that Cometh' and the Divine Name (Apocalypse
1,4.8; 4,8)," *JSJ* 1 (1970) 144-47.
McNamara's treatment of the question is supplemented with non-
targumic material.

176. Ford, J. M. "The Divorce Bill of the Lamb and the Scroll of
the Suspected Adulteress. A Note on Apocalypse 5,1 and 10,8-11,"
JSJ 2 (1971) 136-43.
In the light of the Talmud, the first scroll is a writ of divorce.
The little scroll and the punishment are seen in the light of
Tg. Num 5 and Num R. 9. Rev 17-18 are read in the light of these
Jewish practices. The woman is faithless Jerusalem.

177. Freed, E. D. *Old Testament Quotations in the Gospel of John*
(NovTSup 11; Leiden: Brill, 1965).
A written text of the LXX is the most basic; there also is
evidence of the Hebrew, and of targumic traditions at 6:31, 45;
7:42.

178. Gaston, L. *No Stone on Another. Studies in the Significance
of the Fall of Jerusalem in the Synoptic Gospels* (NovTSup 23;
Leiden: Brill, 1970).
The Tgs. are used in this study only with reference to vocabulary
and ambiguous texts. There is an index.

179. Gerhardsson, B. *The Testing of God's Son. Matthew 4:1-11
and Parallel: An Analysis of an Early Christian Midrash* (ConB NT
Series 2.1; Lund: Gleerup, 1966).
Jewish exegesis of Deut 6--8 lies behind Matt 4:1-11 and Luke
4:1-13 and other NT texts. The MT, LXX and Qumran are used more
than the Tgs. and rabbinic literature. Neof. has not been consulted.

180. Gerhardsson, B. "The Parable of the Sower and its Interpretation
NTS 14 (1968) 165-93.
The parable and its interpretation are constructed in the light of
Jewish exegesis of the Shema (Deut 6:5). The evidence of the Tgs.
and rabbinic literature is only synthesized. Mark 4:10-12 is from
Tg. Isa 6:9-10.

181. Gertner, M. "Midrashim in the New Testament," *JSS* 7 (1962)
267-92.
The apparent lack of coherence in NT texts may be explained as
covert midrashic developments, based on such devices as *'al tiqreh*
and *tartey mišma*^{c}. Four examples are discussed with some use of
the Tgs.: Mark 4:1-22; Luke 1:67-79; 1 Cor 15:55-56; James.

182. Goldberg, A. "Kain: Sohn des Menschen oder Sohn der Schlange?"
Judaica 25 (1969) 203-21.
The tradition preserved in Ps.-J. Gen 4:1-2 concerning the birth of
Cain is early and was excluded by the rabbis for anti-mythical
and anti-mystical reasons. Cf. John 8:44; Matt 3:7.

183. Goldberg, A. *Untersuchungen über die Vorstellung von der
Schekhinah in der frühen rabbinischen Literatur* (Studia Judaica 5;
Berlin: Walter de Gruyter, 1969).
This study is not concerned with the NT, but may provide background
material for John 1:14. The use of the term "Shekinah" may ante-
date the destruction of the temple. Tgs. are not widely used;
see subject index. "Es besteht z. B. eine echte Konkurrenz
zwischen *jekara* im TO und Schekhinah in Talmud und Midrasch
einerseits und in den palastinischen Targumen andererseits" (p. 470).

184. Goldberg, A. M. "Torah aus der Unterwelt? Eine Bemerkung zu
Röm 10,6-7," *B Z* (1970) 127-31.
Paul's use of *abysson* suggests knowledge of the traditions
preserved in Neof., Frg. Deut 30:12-13 and *Pirqe R. El.* 10. An
anti-mystical polemic behind this tradition may also have been
known to Paul.

185. Goodspeed, E. J. "The Possible Aramaic Gospel," *JNES* 1 (1942)
315-40.
Replying to Olmstead, cf. 291, G. denies the early existence of
written Tgs., while admitting oral targumic traditions.

186. Gordon, R. P. "Targumic Parallels to Acts XIII 18 and Didache
XIV 3," *NovT* 16 (1974) 285-89.
Etropophorēsen may reflect the targumic expression *swpyq ṣwrk'*
with reference to God's care of Israel in the desert. There may
be a conflation of the LXX and the Tgs. in Acts 13:18 as in 13:22.
Tg. Mal 1:11 may have influenced *Did.* 14:3; cf. 1 Tim 2:8 and the
notion of spiritual sacrifices in Phil 4:18; Heb 13:15; 1 Pet 2:5;
Rev 8:3, 4.

187. Goulder, M. D. *Midrash and Lection in Matthew* (The Speaker's
Lectures in Biblical Studies 1969-71; London: SPCK, 1974).
Matthew as a Christian scribe has written a midrash on Mark for use
as an annual cycle of readings in conjunction with the synagogue
readings. The use of a Tg. and of targumizing techniques by
Matthew is presupposed. Several possible contacts with the Tgs.
are suggested, but all remain conjectural for G.

188. Grech, P. "Interprophetic Re-interpretation and Old Testament
Eschatology," *AugRom* 9 (1969) 235-65.
The article serves as background material for the NT. The messianic
interpretation of Tg. Isa 14:29 is cited on p. 241.

189. Grelot, P., Pierron, J. *Osternacht und Osterfeier im Alten
und Neuen Bund* (Die Welt der Bibel; Dusseldorf: Patmos, 1959) =
La Nuit et les Fêtes de Pâques (Paris: Ligue Catholique de
l'Evangile, 1956).
Besides the OT, the Mishna, the Talmud, Jubilees, the Pal. Tgs.
and the Mekhilta are considered. Frg. Exod 12:42 is discussed
with reference to the coming of the Messiah on passover night with
reference to Luke 22:14-16; Mark 14:25.

190. Grelot, P. "Les Targums du Pentateuque. Etude comparative
d'après Genèse, IV, 3-16," *Sem* 9 (1959) 59-88.
A hypothetical genealogy of the Tgs. based on a synthetic study
of Tg. Gen 4:3-16. 1 John seems to have known the material in
the Pal. Tg. concerning Cain and Abel.

191. Grelot, P. "'De son ventre couleront des fleuves d'eau.' La
citation scripturaire de Jean VII, 38," *RB* 66 (1959) 369-74.
G. accepts Boismard's proposal concerning *mn gwh*, but contests his
translation of Tg. Ps 78:16. G. examines Jewish traditions
concerning the rock of Num 20, using the Tgs. Cf. 98.

192. Grelot, P. "A propos de Jean VII, 38," *RB* 67 (1960) 224-25.
Corrects citation of Neof. Num 21:16 in an earlier article
(*byrh ḥy'* and not *byrh ḥy'*); cf. 191. Maintains his rejection of
Boismard's translation of Tg. Ps 78:16.

193. Grelot, P. "Etudes néotestamentaires et sources haggadiques,"
Bib 42 (1961) 455-59.
A review article of G. Vermès *Scripture and Tradition in Judaism*
(1961).

194. Grelot, P. "Sagesse 10,21 et le Targum de l'Exode," *Bib* 42
(1961) 49-60.
Wis 10:20-21 reflects Exod 15:1-21 via the Tgs. The long recension
reflects Deut 32:6, 13. Ps.-J. builds on Tg. Ezek 16 which is
applied to Exod 1:15-19. Cf. Ps 8:3. The Pal. Tg. tradition
knew the whole legend.

195. Grelot, P. "Le Messie dans les Apocryphes de l'Ancien Testament. Etat de la question," *La Venue du Messie* (RechBib 6; Bruges: Desclée de Brouwer, 1962) 19-50.
The haggada in the Pal. Tg. of the Pentateuch is fundamentally pre-Christian. The presentation of the Messiah in Pal. Tg. Gen 49:10-12 is parallel to that of Pss. Sol. 17; 18. The Elect One and the Servant are also interpreted messianically in the Tgs.; cf. the Parables of Enoch.

196. Grelot, P. "Jean, VII, 38: Eau du rocher ou source du temple?" *RB* 70 (1963) 43-51.
G. examines Tg. Ezek 47:1-12; Zech 14:8 in search for the citation. *T. Sukk.* III 11-13 recalls the desert rock in association with the feast of Tabernacles. The legend of the rock was born in a targumic milieu. Hypotheses suggested are impossible to verify in present state of knowledge.

197. Grelot, P. "L'exégèse messianique d'Isaïe LXIII, 1-6," *RB* 70 (1963) 371-80.
Rev 19:13, 15 supposes a messianic interpretation of Isa 63:1-6. Such an interpretation appears in Pal. Tg. Gen 49:11 with relics in Tg. Isa 63:2, 6. Rev 19:13, 15 is a Christological application of an already known messianic interpretation of Isa 63:1-6. Some suggestions concerning John 7:27, the hidden Messiah, and the Messiah from Rome.

198. Grimm, W. "Selige Augenzeugen, Luk. 10,23f. Alttestamentlicher Hintergrund und ursprünglicher Sinn," *TZ* 26 (1970) 172-83.
G. looks to Isa 52:13-15 for the explanation of this text. He refers to the Tg. Isa 52:13-15; 35:5; Ps.-J. Num 24:3, 4, 15; Frg. Num 24:3, 15. Implications for other NT texts, esp. 1 Cor 2:7-10; Luke 2:25-32; John 8:56; 12:40-41; Matt 13:16, 17.

199. Guilding, A. *The Fourth Gospel and Jewish Worship. A Study of the relation of St. John's Gospel to the ancient Jewish lectionary system* (Oxford: Clarendon, 1960).
The structure of the Fourth Gospel and the teaching of Jesus contained therein are based on a three year cycle of *sedarim* and *haptaroth* (beginning in Nisan; but also in Tishri after 70 A. D.). References are made to the Tgs. esp. concerning John 6--9.

200. Gundry, R. H. *The Use of the Old Testament in St. Matthew's Gospel. With Special Reference to the Messianic Hope* (NovTSup 18; Leiden: Brill, 1967).

Matthew, a note-taker during the life of Jesus, dealt with the OT
in a targumizing manner. Direct influence of the Tgs. is detected
in many places.

201. Hanson, A. T. *Studies in Paul's Technique and Theology* (London:
SPCK, 1974).
Seven independent studies on various themes, followed by five
chapters on the implications of these studies for Paul's theology,
with special reference to his use of the OT. Paul's OT texts are
investigated in the light of Jewish tradition before Paul's
christological interpretation is explored. An index refers to the
use made of the Tgs.

202. Harmon, A.   "Aspects of Paul's Use of the Psalms," *WTJ* 32
(1970) 1-23.
On pp. 5-7, H. discusses the possible influence of Tg Ps 68:18 on
Eph 4:8. He concludes that a citation cannot be substantiated.
Paul may have been familiar with a Jewish interpretation, but more
likely has deliberately altered the text to bring out the full
meaning of the passage.

203. Hayward, R.   "The Memra of YHWH and the Development of its
Use in Targum Neofiti I," *JJS* 25 (1974) 412-18.
A criticism of Muñoz León's thesis. The evidence of Neof. Deut
indicates that Neof. m. is an outgrowth of Neof. "Name of the
Memra" came to be used in place of an earlier and sparing use,
reflecting a particular and distinctive theology of the divine Name
and Presence. Memra gradually became a mere substitute for Yahweh,
leading to the loss of a rich and fertile idea in Jewish exegesis.

204. Hengel , M. *Judentum und Hellenismus. Studien zu ihrer
Begegnung unter besonderer Berücksichtigung Palästinas bis zur Mitte
des Jh. vor Christus* (WUNT 10; Tübingen: Mohr, 1st ed. 1969; 2nd
revised and enlarged ed. 1973). ET: *Judaism and Hellenism. Studies
in their Encounter in Palestine during the Early Hellenistic
Period* 2 vols. (Philadelphia: Fortress, 1974; translated from the
2nd German ed.).
This study does not deal directly with the NT. There are a few
references to the Tgs. and a Targum index.

205. Hickling, C. "The Sequence of Thought in II Corinthians
Chapter Three," *NTS* 21 (1975) 380-95.
2 Cor 3:7 and Neof. gl. Exod 34:29. 2 Cor 3:10-15 and Exod 34:29-35.
H. is hesitant about McNamara's and Le Déaut's use of Ps.-J. Exod
33:7-8 with reference to 2 Cor 7:16 (*epistrepsē*).

206. Hillyer, N. "The Servant of God," *EvQ* 41 (1969) 143-60.
A good summary of Jewish material in accessible form. Treats the
binding of Isaac in Judaism (pp. 144-48); the binding of Isaac
and the suffering servant (pp. 148-51; cf. 11QtgJob 3:18; Pal. Tg.
Gen 22:8; Lev 22:27); the binding of Isaac in the NT (pp. 151-57).

207. Isenberg, S. "An Anti-Sadducee Polemic in the Palestinian
Targum Tradition," *HTR* 63 (1970) 433-44.
Cain's rejection of the future world in Ps.-J., Neof. Gen 4:3-16.

208. Jacobs, I. "The Midrashic Background for James II.21-3," *NTS*
22 (1976) 457-64.
The evidence of the Apocrypha, Tgs., Philo, and *Bib. Ant.* as
background for Jas 2:21-23.

209. Jaubert, A. *La notion d'Alliance dans le Judaïsme aux abords
de l'ère chrétienne* (Patristica Sorbonensia 6; Paris: Seuil, 1963).
Very little attention is given to rabbinic literature and the Tgs.
are not used at all.

210. Jaubert, A. "La symbolique du puits de Jacob," *L'Homme devant
Dieu. Mélanges H. de Lubac I* (Théologie 56: Paris: Aubier, 1963)
63-73.
Jewish tradition concerning wells. The article includes an
examination of the targumic material concerning the wells of the
Patriarchs, and especially the well of Jacob. Besides John 4, cf.
also 1 Cor 10:4.

211. Jaubert, A. "Les séances du sanhédrin et les récits de la
passion," *RHR* 166 (1964) 143-69; 167 (1965) 1-33.
The rules of the Pal. Tgs. are used for the first time to determine
the Jewish law under which the Sanhedrin may have tried Jesus.
Ps.-J., Frg., and Neof. Lev 24:12; Num 9:8; 15:34; 27:5 and the
four judgments of Moses. This evidence supports the long chronology
of the passion.

212. Jaubert, A. "Symboles et figures dans le judaïsme," *RevScRel*
47 (1973) 373-90.
A popular presentation of other research concerning the importance
of Jewish biblical interpretation for NT exegesis. Three examples
are presented: (1) the figure of the stone; (2) traditions concerning Moses; (3) Isaac and the Akedah.

213. Jeremias, J. *Die Abendmahlsworte Jesu* (Göttingen: Vandenhoeck
und Ruprecht, 1st ed. 1935; 2nd ed. 1949; 3rd ed. 1960; 4th ed.

1967).   ET: *The Eucharistic Words of Jesus* (London: SCM, 1966;
translated from the 3rd German ed. with the author's revisions to
July 1964).
The Tgs. are used primarily to illustrate Jewish passover
vocabulary related to the last supper accounts of the NT.   There
is a Targum index in the 3rd German edition.

214.   Johnson, M. D. *The Purpose of Biblical Genealogies* (SNTSMS;
Cambridge, Mass.: University Press, 1969).
Notice is taken of R. Bloch's article concerning Tamar, but more
weight is given to later rabbinic tradition which was critical of
Tamar's place in David's genealogy.

215.   Jousse, M. *Les Formules targoûmiques du "Pater" dans le
Milieu ethnique palestinien* (Paris: Geuthner, 1944).
An anthropologist criticizes the Greco-Latin approach to texts of
Palestinian origin.   The oral targumic tradition needs to be
considered.   Parallel passages to the "Our Father" are cited from
the extant Tgs. (pp. 39-42) and a rhythmic Aramaic translation of
the "Our Father" is presented.

216.   Kahle, P. "Das palästinische Pentateuchtargum und das zur
Zeit Jesu gesprochene Aramäisch," *ZNW* 49 (1958) 100-16.
K. deals with the present state of targumic studies, defends the
early origin of the Pal. Tgs., and expresses reserves concerning
Kutscher's position on Palestinian Aramaic.   Kahle recognizes only
one form of Palestinian Aramaic, with differences in pronunciation
between Galilee and Judaea.

217.   Kahle, P. *The Cairo Geniza* (Schweich Lectures 1941; London:
Oxford University Press, 1947; 2nd ed. Oxford: Blackwell, 1959).
The second edition takes account of Qumran and Neofiti 1, esp. in
chaps. 2--3.   The material and language of the Pal. Tgs. belong to
Christian and pre-Christian times.   More is to be learned from the
Tgs. about 1st cent. Judaism than Billerbeck and Bonsirven allow.

218.   Kelly, J. N. D.   *A Commentary on the Epistles of Peter and of
Jude* (London: Adam and Charles Black, 1969).
The Tgs. are used with reference to Cain (Jude 11, 12; pp. 267, 273)
and 1 Pet 1:3; 3:20.

219.   Koch, K. "Das Lamm, das Aegypten vernichtet. Ein Fragment aus
Jannes und Jambres und sein geschichtlicher Hintergrund," *ZNW* 57
(1966) 79-93.

Jannes and Jambres in 2 Tim 3:8 and Ps.-J. Exod 1:15; 7:11; Num
22:22; CD 5:17-19. Moses as a lamb may be derived from a 7th-8th
cent. A. D. demotic papyrus concerning the prophecy of a Syrian
invasion of Egypt under Bokharis. K. sees this as evidence for a
pre-Christian use of "lamb" as "redeemer" against Jeremias.

220. Koch, K. "Messias und Sündenvergebung in Jesaja 53--Targum.
Ein Beitrag zu der Praxis der aramäischen Bibelübersetzung,"
JSJ 3 (1972) 117-48.
Tg. Isa 53 is pre-Christian and based on a Hebrew text which differs
from the MT.

221. Kosmala, H. "Matthew xxvi 52--A Quotation from the Targum,"
NovT 4 (1960) 3-5.
Matt 26:52 is a modified translation of Tg. Isa 50:11, implying a
divine verdict with eschatological implications. Cf. Rev 17:8.

222. Lapide, P. "Insights from Qumran into the Languages of Jesus,"
RQ 8 (1972-75) 483-501.
Qumran supports the trilingual situation of Palestine in Jesus'
time. Pp. 496-97 discuss the Hebrew and Aramaic possibilities of
Matt 27:46; Mark 15:34.

223. Laurentin, R. *Structure et théologie de Luc I-II* (EB; Paris:
Gabalda, 1957).
L. disagrees with Winter's interpretation of Luke 2:49 based on
Frg. Exod 15:2 (pp. 141-46). He refers to Ps.-J. Gen 35:21 with
reference to Luke 2:1-14 and Mic 4:7-10 concerning the manifestation
of the Messiah (p. 87).

224. Le Déaut, R. "Traditions targumiques dans le Corpus Paulinien?
(Hebr 11, 4 et 12,24; Gal 4,29-30; II Cor 3,16)," *Bib* 42 (1961)
28-48.
The Pal. Tgs. presentation of Cain and Abel in Gen 4:8; Ishmael's
contestation with Isaac in Gen 22:1; and the conversion of Israel
in Exod 33:7-12 may illuminate the NT presentation of Cain and
Abel, Gal 4:29-30, and 2 Cor 3:16.

225. Le Déaut, R. "Le Targum de Gen. 22,8 et 1 Pt. 1,20," *RSR* 49
(1961) 103-106.
The Tgs. of Gen 22:8, 13 may explain the divine foreknowledge of
the paschal victim in 1 Pet 1:20.

226. Le Déaut, R. "Goûter le calice de la mort," *Bib* 43 (1962)
82-86.
The expression "to taste the cup of death" may appear in Neof. Deut
32:1 (if not a misreading for "the poison of death"). If so, the
expression is reflected in Matt 20:22-23; 26:28; Mark 10:38-39;
John 18:11.

227. Le Déaut, R. "Pentecôte et tradition juive," *Spiritus* no. 7
(1961) 127-44; *AsSeign* no. 51 (1963) 22-38; *Doctrine and Life* 20
(1970) 257-67.
Modifications in the Jewish understanding of the feast of Weeks
from pre-Christian to later rabbinic times. Association of the
feast with the covenant and the gift of the Law may be pre-Christian
and more closely associated with Passover at this earlier date.
These traditions are significant for the NT understanding of the
glorification of Jesus, and the gift of the Spirit as the New Law
of the new *ekklēsia*.

228. Le Déaut, R. "La présentation targumique du sacrifice d'Isaac
et la sotériologie paulinienne," *Studiorum paulinorum congressus
internationalis catholicus* (AnBib 17-18; Rome: Pontifical Biblical
Institute, 1963) 563-74.
Most of the midrashic material concerning the sacrifice of Isaac
can be found in the Tg. Gen 22. These traditions were known to
Philo, Josephus, and Pseudo-Philo, and may have been associated
with Passover at an early date. The Akedah did not profoundly
influence Paul's theology, but the sacrifice of Jesus may have been
contrasted with that of Isaac in the matter of expiation.

229. Le Déaut, R. "De nocte paschatis," *VD* 41 (1963) 189-95.
A summary of his dissertation; cf. 230.

230. Le Déaut, R. *La Nuit Pascale. Essai sur la signification de
la Pâque juive à partir du Targum d'Exode XII 42* (AnBib 22; Rome:
Institut Biblique Pontifical, 1963; photographic reprint 1975).
A thorough study of the Jewish traditions contained in the poem of
the "Four Nights" (Pal. Tgs. Exod 12:42) with an introduction to
targumic literature. The tradition which expected the Messiah on
the 15th of Nisan is pre-Christian and influenced the NT theology
of the redemption.

231. Le Déaut, R. "Miryam, soeur de Moïse, mère du Messie," *Bib*
45 (1964) 198-219.

A review of Jewish traditions concerning Miryam from the OT to the
Midrashim, including the Tgs. These traditions should be considered
in evaluating the NT treatment of Mary alongside Jesus, the new
Moses.

232. Le Déaut, R. "Actes 7,48 et Matthieu 17,4 (par.) à la lumière
du Targum Palestinien," *RSR* 52 (1964) 85-90.
Ps.-J. and Neof. m. Exod 39:43, concerning the dwelling place of
the Shekinah in "the work of your hands," emphasizes the scandal
of Stephen's words in Acts 7:48. The cloud of glory and the
presence of God are associated with Tabernacles in Tg. Exod 13:20;
Lev 23:42. The NT must be understood in the light of these
haggadic traditions.

233. Le Déaut, R. "Marie et l'Ecriture dans le Chapitre VIII (i.e.
of the Dogmatic Constitution *Lumen Gentium*)," *Etudes Mariales* 22
(1965) 55-74.
The article mentions Tg. Zech 3:14-17 with reference to Mary as
the Daughter of Sion in Luke 1:35; cf. also John 1:14 (p. 65).
The Word of God must be seen in the living interpretation of
tradition.

234. Le Déaut, R. *Liturgie juive et Nouveau Testament. Le
Témoignage des versions araméenes* (Rome: Institut Biblique
Pontifical, 1965).
A popular presentation of the significance of recent targumic
studies for a knowledge of the inter-relationship of the synagogue
and the early church.

235. Le Déaut, R. *Introduction à la littérature targumique.
Première partie* (ad usum privatum; Rome: Institut Biblique
Pontifical, 1966).
A student's manual dealing with the history of the Aramaic versions,
extant texts, dating and methodology for the history of Jewish
exegesis and NT interpretation. Bibliographies in the footnotes.

236. Le Déaut, R. "Le substrat araméen des évangiles: scolies en
marge de l'Aramaic Approach de Matthew Black," *Bib* 49 (1968)
388-99.
A review article of the 3rd ed. of M. Black, *An Aramaic Approach to
the Gospels and Acts*. L. adds much new evidence from Neof.

237. Le Déaut, R. "Les études targumiques. Etat de la recherche
et perspectives pour l'exégèse de l'Ancien Testament," *ETL* 44
(1968) 5-34.

A thorough review with bibliographies of contemporary targumic
studies as significant for OT textual criticism and the Jewish
understanding of Scripture in the intertestamental period.

238. Le Déaut, R. "Tradition juive et exégèse chrétienne," *Jalones
de la Historia de la Salvación en el Antiguo y Nuevo Testamento*
(26 Semana Biblica Española 1965; Madrid: CSIC, 1969) II 7-33.
The importance of studying the living tradition of the Jewish
biblical interpretation for understanding the use of the OT in the
NT. Many examples are included.

239. Le Déaut, R. "Première Pâque en Terre promise (Jos 5,9a.10-12),"
AsSeign no. 17 (1969) 52-57.
The conversion of Israel and the return to the Law in Neof. Josh
5:9; the blood of the Passover and the blood of circumcision are
both associated with salvation. The Eucharist is prefigured by the
manna, not by the paschal lamb (cf. John 6; 1 Cor 10:3). Heb 3-4
speak of entering the rest of God under the leadership of the new
Joshua.

240. Le Déaut, R. "Les études targumiques. Etat de la recherche et
perspectives pour l'exégèse de l'Ancien Testament," *Donum Natalicium
J. Coppens...*(ed. H. Cazelles) Vol. I: *De Mari à Qumrân. L'Ancien
Testament. Son Milieu. Ses Ecrits. Ses Relectures Juives*
(Gembloux/Paris: Duculot/Lethielleux, 1969) 302-31.
A review of targumic studies and their importance prior to and
since 1930. The liturgical origin of the targumic tradition.
Targumism defies the critical dictum, *lectio difficilior potior*.

241. Le Déaut, R. "Pâque juive et Nouveau Testament," *Studies on
the Jewish Background of the New Testament* (Articles by O. Michel,
S. Safrai, R. Le Déaut, M. de Jonge, J. van Goudoever; Assen: Van
Gorcum, 1969) 22-43.
Common traits in Jewish paschal theology and Christian paschal
theology. Considerable use is made of the Tgs.

242. Le Déaut, R. "Une aggadah targumique et les 'murmures' de
Jean 6," *Bib* 51 (1970) 80-83.
Comments on Malina's 1968 study of the manna tradition. Ps.-J.
Num 11:6-7 should read *ḥywr* (white) and *qryš* (solidified). The Tg.
is a protest against the scandalous ingratitude of Israel (cf.
John 6:41-43, 58-61).

243. Le Déaut, R. "Aspects de l'intercession dans le Judaïsme
ancien," *JSJ* 1 (1970) 35-57.

The notion of intercession in intertestamental Judaism is presented as background for the NT. The latter is not treated explicitly.

244. Le Déaut, R. "A propos d'une définition du midrash," *Bib* 50 (1969) 395-413 = "Apropos a Definition of Midrash," *Int* 25 (1971) 259-82.
A. G. Wright's definition of "midrash" as a literary genre is not broad enough to deal with the historical development of biblical interpretation in Judaism and its influence on the NT.

245. Le Déaut, R. "La tradition juive ancienne et l'exégèse chrétienne primitive," *RHPR* 51 (1971) 31-50.
The importance of knowing the living tradition of the Jewish understanding of Scripture for the student of the NT and the early church. A review of scholarship concerning targumic and midrashic traditions.

246. Le Déaut, R. "Un phénomène spontané de l'herméneutique juive ancienne: le 'targuisme'," *Bib* 52 (1971) 505-25.
The Tgs., as liturgical translations, form a link between the biblical texts and the more elaborate Midrashim. They bear witness to the living interpretation and actualizing of Scripture among the Jews.

247. Le Déaut, R. "The Current State of Targumic Studies," *BTB* 4 (1974) 3-32.
Targumic studies since Kahle. The present state of editorial work. Emerging issues.

248. Le Déaut, R. "Targumic Literature and New Testament Interpretation," *BTB* 4 (1974) 243-89.
A review of recent work, with cautions and new suggestions.

249. Le Déaut, R. "Les targums ou versions araméenes de la Bible," *SIDIC* 9 (2, 1976) 4-11.
Introductory information with NT examples already treated elsewhere.

249a. Le Déaut, R., Robert J. *Targum du Pentateuque*. Traduction des deux recensions palestiniennes complètes avec introduction, parallèles, notes et index. Tome I. *Genèse*. Tome II. *Exode-Lévitique*. Tome III. *Nombres-Deutéronome* (SC 245- ; Paris: Cerf, 1978-).

250. Lehmann, C. *Auferweckt am dritten Tag nach der Schrift. Exegetische und fundamentaltheologische Studien* (Quaestiones Disputatae 38; Freiburg im Br.: Herder, 1968).

The study seeks to discover a theological significance to "the
third day" in Jewish tradition. See Ps.-J. Gen 22:1. Pp. 262-90
consider the contribution of the Tgs. and the Midrashim to the
elucidation of 1 Cor 15:4b.

251. Lentzen-Deis, F. *Die Taufe Jesu nach den Synoptikern* (Frank-
furter Theologische Studien 4; Frankfurt am Main: J. Knecht, 1970).
The Tgs. are used throughout to elucidate the Jewish traditions
lying behind the NT presentation of John's baptism and the theophany
at the baptism of Jesus. Targumic texts, esp. Tg. Gen 15; 22 are
used to isolate a literary form called a "Deute-Vision" (chap.5),
which is then applied to the NT baptismal theophany (chap. 6).

252. Levey, S. H. *The Messiah: An Aramaic Interpretation. The
Messianic Exegesis of the Targum* (Monographs of the Hebrew Union
College 2; Cincinnati/Jerusalem: HUC Press, 1974).
An English translation and critical examination of messianic texts
in the MT and the Tgs., with reference to the LXX, Vulgate, and
Syriac. Summaries conclude the treatment of the Pentateuch,
Prophets, and Hagiographa as well as the whole study. An index
lists 13 NT texts cited in the course of the work. The author
knows of Neofiti 1 but does not use it.

253. Lewis, J. P. *A Study of the Interpretation of Noah and the
Flood in Jewish and Christian Literature* (Leiden: Brill, 1968).
The Tgs. are considered to reflect rabbinic, rather than earlier,
traditions.

254. Lipinski, E. "Etudes sur des textes 'messianiques' de l'Ancien
Testament," *Sem* 20 (1970) 41-57.
L. rejects an individual messianic interpretation of the woman's
descendants in Tg. Gen 3:14-15 and any notion of a definitive
victory.

255. Lövestam, E. *Son and Saviour. A Study of Acts 13:32-37. With
an Appendix: 'Son of God' in the Synoptic Gospels (ConNT* 18; Lund:
Gleerup, 1961).
The messianic interpretation of Tg. Ps 80:16; cf. Tg. Ps 2:7. The
Tgs. and Midrashim soften the suggestion of *divine* sonship; cf.
Tg. 2 Sam 7:14; Pss 2:7; 89:28. Tgs. are also cited with reference
to Acts 2:24; 13:34.

256. Luzárraga, J. *Las Tradiciones de la Nube en la Biblia y en
el Judaismo primitivo* (AnBib 54; Rome: Pontifical Biblical
Institute, 1973).

The author studies the "cloud" vocabulary of the OT and the
midrashic development of its symbolism to the end of the Amoraic
period. The significance of these traditions for NT texts concerning
the transfiguration, the ascension, and eschatology are particularly
developed. An appendix deals with the Holy Spirit and the Church.

257. Luzárraga, J. "Fondo targumico del cuarto evangelio," *EstE*
49 (1974) 251-63.
L. pleads for a wider use of the Pal. Tgs. in the study of John.
Many illustrations.

258. Luzárraga, J. "Presentación de Jesús a la luz del Antiguo
Testamento en el Evangelio de Juan," *EstE* 51 (1976) 497-520.
The targumizing interpretation of the synagogue is presupposed in
John 6:31; 8:56; 12:40; 3:14-15. In the NT, the OT is interiorized
with Jesus as the catalyst.

259. Lyonnet, S. "Saint Paul et l'exégèse juive de son temps. A
propos de Rom.,10,6-8," *Mélanges bibliques redigés en l'honneur
d'André Robert* (Paris: Bloud & Gay, 1957) 494-506.
After presenting a history of recent exegesis, L. applies Frg. Deut
30:12-13 to the elucidation of the text. Paul's awareness of
targumic traditions is also apparent in 1 Cor 10:4; Eph 4:8; 2
Tim 3:8.

260. Lyonnet, S. "Péché. III Dans le Judaïsme. IV Dans le Nouveau
Testament," *DBSup* VII 481-68 (Paris: Letouzey et Ané, 1964).
Concupiscence in Tg. Gen 3:6; Adam in the garden to observe the
Law (Tg. Gen 2:15), which is described as a tree of life (Tg. Gen
3:23).

261. Lyonnet, S. "L'histoire du salut selon le chapitre VII de
l'épître aux Romains," *Bib* 43 (1962) 117-51.
Rom 7 is based on a reading of Gen 1-3. According to Neof. Gen
2:15 Adam is put in paradise to observe the Law; the Law is associated
with the tree of life in Neof. Gen 3:23; cf. Rom 7;12. Concupiscence
in a general sense is "sin" par excellence; cf. the absolute use of
ḥmd in Neof. Exod 20:17; Deut 5:18; Gen 3:6; cf. Rom 7:7.

262. Lyonnet, S. "'Tu ne convoiteras pas' (Rom. vii 7)," *Neotestamentica et Patristica* (Festschrift O. Cullmann; Leiden: Brill, 1962)
154-65.
The absolute use of the verb "to covet" (ḥmd) in the Tgs. indicates
that Paul still has Gen 2-3 in mind at Rom 7:7. Cf. also 1 Cor 10:6;
Col 3:5; Eph 5:5.

263. Lyonnet, S. *Exegesis Epistulae ad Romanos. Cap. I ad IV.*
Editio Tertia Recognita at Aucta. Ad usum privatum auditorum
(Rome: Pontificium Institutum Biblicum, 1963).
Tgs. are used with reference to the use of *agapētos* for the elect
people; Rom 3:5, 23; 4:3, 15, 17b, 20; cf. Gal 4:29; Eph 4:8;
1 Cor 10:4; 2 Tim 3:8.

264. Lyonnet, S. *Exegesis Epistulae ad Romanos. Cap. V ad VIII*
(Except. Rom 5, 12-21). Editio altera recognita. Ad usum privatum
auditorum. (Rome: Pontificium Institutum Biblicum, 1966).
Pauline dependence on Tgs. at Rom 7:7b, 9, 17; 8:9-10, 15, 32.

265. Lyonnet, S. *Quaestiones in Epistulam ad Romanos. Series
Altera. Rom 9--11.* Editio tertia cum Supplemento. Ad usum
privatum (Rome: Pontificium Institutum Biblicum, 1975).
Pauline dependence on Tgs. at Rom 10:6-8; 11:9; 12:19; 1 Cor 10:4;
Eph 4:8; 2 Tim 3:8.

266. McArthur, H. "'On the Third Day'," *NTS* 18 (1972) 81-86.
Tg. Hos 6:2 understands the resurrection of the dead; the eschatological character of the text is maintained in rabbinic literature
and connected with the Jonah episode (cf. Matt 12:40). There is
no contrary evidence for an early date for the resurrection
interpretation of Hos 6:2; cf. NT texts concerning the resurrection
"on the third day" or "after three days."

267. McNamara, M. *The New Testament and the Palestinian Targum to
the Pentateuch* (AnBib 27; Rome: Pontifical Biblical Institute,
1966).
A history of targumic studies with bibliographies. Present
problems and recent work. A detailed examination of the use already
made of the Tgs. in NT interpretation, new proposals and suggestions
for new work.

268. McNamara, M. "The Aramaic Translations: A Newly Discovered Aid
for New Testament Study," *Scr* 18 (1966) 47-56 = *Irish Ecclesiastical
Record* 109 (1968) 158-65.
A general introduction to the study of the Tgs. and a suggestion of
their use in NT study.

269. McNamara, M. "Targumic Studies," *CBQ* 28 (1966) 1-19.
Targumic studies from the late Middle Ages to the present day with
bibliographies. Significance for the NT. Important scholars and
studies.

270. McNamara, M. "Jewish Liturgy and the New Testament," *TBT* no. 33 (1967) 2324-32.
A number of NT texts are discussed in the light of such targumic notions as the Glory of the Shekinah of Yahweh, the Memra of Yahweh, the spirit, redemption and the days of the Messiah.

271. McNamara, M. "*Logos* of the Fourth Gospel and *Memra* of the Palestinian Targum (Ex 12:42)," *ExpTim* 79 (1968) 115-17.
A brief history of the scholarship. Rev and Jewish liturgy. The Word of God in the prologue of John and the Tgs.; light and darkness in the Tgs. and the Johannine literature. Jewish liturgy is more important for the NT than Qumran.

272. McNamara, M. *Targum and Testament. Aramaic Paraphrases of the Hebrew Bible. A Light on the New Testament* (Grand Rapids/Shannon: Eerdmans/Irish University Press, 1972).
An introduction for non-specialists to recent developments in targumic studies, including their use in NT exegesis. The book contains an introduction to all extant targumic texts.

273. McNeil, B. "The Quotation at John XII 34," *NovT* 19 (1977) 22-33.
M. proposes a text of Isa 9:5 which approximates the Tg., thus avoiding the danger of angel-christology suggested by the LXX.

274. Maher, M. "Some Aspects of Torah in Judaism," *ITQ* 38 (1971) 310-25.
Recent work on the Tgs. is abundantly used in this provisional synthesis of Jewish attitudes to the Law and their influence on the development of christology in the NT.

275. Malina, B. "Matthew 2 and Is 41,2-3: a Possible Relationship?" *SBFLA* 17 (1967) 291-302.
Matt 2 may be a midrash on Tg. Isa 41:2-3: "Who openly led forth from the East Abraham, the chosen one of the just; in truth he drew him near to his place ..." Cf. also Tg. Isa 43:11; 48:15-16.

276. Malina, B. *The Palestinian Manna Tradition. The Manna Tradition in the Palestinian Targums and its Relationship to the New Testament* (Arbeiten zur Geschichte des späteren Judentums und des Urchristentums 7; Leiden: Brill, 1968).
The development of the manna tradition in the OT and the Pal. Tgs. These traditions throw light on many NT texts, esp. John 6; 1 Cor 10:3; Rev 2:17; Matt 4:4; 1 Pet 1:20; Heb 9:4.

277. Malina, B. "Some Observations on the Origins of Sin in Judaism
and Saint Paul," *CBQ* 31 (1969) 18-34.
The primary focus of the article is on the OT, Apocrypha and
Pseudepigrapha, and rabbinic literature. Sammaël ("the poison of
God") in Ps.-J. Gen 3:6 and his responsibility for the *yeṣer hara^c*
in man are mentioned on pp. 25-26. Cf. Rom 5:12-21.

278. Manns, F. "Un hymne judéo-chrétien: Philippiens 2,6-11,"
EuntDoc 29 (1976) 259-90.
The humiliation-exaltation structure of 1 Sam 2:7-10 and its
messianic interpretation of Tg. Isa 52:13--53:12, but esp. Tg. Isa
45:23 and Phil 2:11. The speeches of Acts may reflect Tgs. in their
lack of emphasis on expiation, and their insistence on the purification and restoration of the community.

279. Manns, F. *"La vérité vous fera libres."* Etude exégétique de
Jean 8/31-59 (Studium Biblicum Franciscanum Analecta 11; Jerusalem:
Franciscan Printing Press, 1976).
The paternity of Abraham in Jewish tradition is discussed with
special reference to Tg. Gen 15; the paternity of the devil with
special reference to Tg. Gen 3--4. John 8:31-59 is a Christian
midrash on these themes with the help of Jewish tradition on Ps 118
(see Tg.) and the feast of Tabernacles. The book contains a Targum
index.

280. Marzotto, D. "Giovanni 17 e il Targum di Esodo 19-20," *RivB* 25
(1977) 375-88.
M. presupposes Potin's work on Tg. Exod 19--20 and a covenant
context for John 17. Jesus and Moses are both mediators of the
revelation of God himself. Implications for unity.

281. Miller, M. P. "Targum, Midrash and the Use of the Old Testament
in the New Testament," *JSJ* 2 (1971) 29-82.
The state of the question to date. Good bibliographies.

282. Morag, S. "'Ephphatha' (Mark VII.34)- Certainly Hebrew, Not
Aramaic?" *JSS* 17 (1972) 198-202.
Evidence from the oral Samaritan tradition for the assimilation of
t, against Rabinowitz. Aramaic as likely as Hebrew.

283. Muñoz Iglesias, S. "Midráš y Evangelios de la Infancia,"
EstE 47 (1972) 331-59.
M. takes a position with Le Déaut against Wright.

284. Muñoz León, D. "La esperanza de Israel. Perspectivas de la espera mesiánica en los targumín palestinenses del Pentateuco," *30 Semana Bíblica Española* (Madrid: CSIC, 1972) 49-91.
Messianic and eschatological interpretations in the Pal. Tgs. to the Pentateuch, esp. Neof. Selected texts and a synthesis in relation to NT realization.

285. Muñoz León, D. "La Palabra de Dios y el testimonio de Jesucristo: Una nueva interpretación de la fórmula en el Apocalipsis," *EstBíb* 31 (1972) 179-99.
Christians bear witness to Jesus as Word of God by the force of the Spirit. Pal. Tg. Gen 3:15 is mentioned once (p. 186).

286. Muñoz León, D. *Dios-Palabra. Memrá en los Targumim del Pentateuco* (Institución San Jeronimo 4; Granada: Editorial Santa Rita, 1974).
The first of three volumes. Memra is not an automatic liturgical substitute for the divine Name nor an hypostasis. It connotes the divine action in terms of God's creating, revealing and saving word. The expression becomes a theological denomination for God himself and prepares later Judaism and the NT.

287. Muñoz León, D. "Adoración en espíritu y verdad. Aportación targúmica a la inteligencia de Jn 4,23-24," *Homenaje a Juan Prado. Miscelanea de Estudios Bíblicos y Hebraicos* (edd. L. Alvarez Verdes, E. J. Alonso Hernandez; Madrid: CSIC, 1975) 387-403.
Pal. Tgs. render "to walk with God" as "to offer a cult in truth." In John, authentic cult is a gift of the Spirit.

288. Muñoz León, D. *Gloria de la Shekina en los Targumim del Pentateuco* (Madrid: CSIC, 1977).

289. Nickels, P. *Targum and New Testament. A Bibliography together with a New Testament Index* (Rome: Pontifical Biblical Institute, 1967).
A bibliography of 36 books and 88 articles. The NT index contains 759 entries with brief annotations concerning significant contributions from Aramaic and targumic studies.

290. O'Hagan, A. "The First Christian Pentecost (Acts 2:1-13)," *SBFLA* 23 (1973) 50-66.
The exegesis of Acts 2:1-13 is followed by historical considerations. Context of the Sinai covenant and the constitution of the people of God. Jewish association of Pentecost and covenant

directly attested by 150 A. D., indirectly by 100 A. D.   Evidence
of the Tgs. and NT texts.

291. Olmstead, A. "Could an Aramaic Gospel be Written?" *JNES* 1
(1942) 41-75.
Against Goodspeed, O. puts forth evidence for the existence of
Aramaic gospels, affirming a pre-Christian date for written Tgs.
He would use the language of the Tgs., esp. in editions and sections
which can be shown to be pre-Christian.

292. Olsson, B. *Structure and Meaning in the Fourth Gospel. A
Text-Linguistic Analysis of John 2:1-11 and 4:1-42* (ConB NT Series
6; Lund: Gleerup, 1974).
The Tgs. are extensively used to illustrate the traditions contained
in these two pericopes.   The Targum index is not complete.

293. Ott, H. "Um die Muttersprache Jesu.   Forschungen seit Gustaf
Dalman," *NovT* 9 (1967) 1-25.
Review of scholarship to date.

294. Panimolle, S. *Il dono della Legge e la grazia della verità
(Gv 1,17)* (Rome: A.V.E., 1973).
Qumran and the Tgs. are used to reach a deeper understanding of
charis kai alētheia.

295. Patsch, H. "Zum alttestamentlichen Hintergrund von Römer 4:25
und I.Petrus 2:24," *ZNW* 60 (1969) 273-79.
A critical examination of the use made of Tg. Isa 53:5b, 12 to
explain Rom 4:25; 1 Cor 15:3.   The plural of "sins" in 1 Pet 2:24
can be found in a pre-Masoretic form at Qumran, in the Tgs., and
in other versions.

296. Paul, A. *L'Evangile de l'enfance selon saint Matthieu* (Paris:
Cerf, 1968).
The Tgs. are mentioned with respect to the four women in Matt 1.
Tg. Num 24:17, 7 are discussed in relation to Matt 2.

297. Perez Fernández, M. "'prope est aestas' (Mc 13,28; Mt 24,32;
Lc 21,29)," *VD* 46 (1968) 361-69.
P. is dependent on Gertner's study of midrashim in the NT.   An *'al
tiqrey* interpretation of the Aramaic *q(y)ṣ* explains the NT formula;
cf. Tgs. Gen 49:1; Jer 8:20.

298. Perrot, C. "La lecture de la Bible dans les synagogues au
premier siècle de notre ère," *Maison-Dieu* no. 126 (1976) 24-41.

The present state of knowledge concerning the synagogue readings
in the 1st cent. A. D.   Pp. 34-38 list the *sedarim* and *haptaroth*.

299. Perrot, C. "La lecture synagogale d'Exode XXI,1--XXII,23 et son
influence sur la littérature néo-testamentaire," *A la rencontre de
Dieu. Mémorial A. Gélin* (Le Puy/Lyon/Paris: Xavier Mappus, 1961)
223-39.
The corresponding *haptarah* was Isa 56:1-9; 57:19. The corresponding
Targums and extant homilies are discussed with reference to NT texts.

300. Perrot, C. *Pseudo-Philon. Les Antiquités Bibliques.* Tome II.
Introduction littéraire, commentaire et index (SC 230; Paris:
Cerf, 1976) 10-65.
P. discusses the content, literary form, purpose, origin and
theological thought of the Biblical Antiquities. The work is
neither a targum nor an exegetical midrash, but rather a popular
midrash.

301. Perrot, C. "Les récits d'enfance dans la haggada antérieure au
II siècle de notre ère," *RSR* 55 (1967) 481-518.
The Tgs. and Midrashim are used in a complementary fashion.

302. Perrot, C. "Luc 4,16-30 et la lecture biblique de l'ancienne
synagogue," *RevScRel* 47 (1973) 324-40 = *Exégèse biblique et Judaïsme*
(ed. J.-E. Ménard; Leiden: Brill, 1973) 170-83.
Synagogue readings, homiletic forms, and associations in the Tgs.
help to explain the text of Luke 4:16-30.

303. Potin, J. *La fête juive de la Pentecôte* (LD 65; Paris: Cerf,
1971).
A critical study of the Tgs. of Exod 19--20 and the Jewish synagogue
liturgy of Weeks as a background for the Lucan narrative of Acts 2.
The covenant was primarily remembered in the Essene and priestly
tradition; the emphasis shifted to the giving of the Law with the
rabbis. Tg. Hab 3; Ezek 1; Pss 29; 68; 77; 18; Deut 16; Exod 24
are also studied in the same context. The final chapter deals with
Acts 2 and an appendix with John 1:19--2:12. A second volume
contains the Aramaic texts.

304. Rabinowitz, I. "'Be opened' = Ephphatha (Mark 7:34): Did
Jesus Speak Hebrew?" *ZNW* 53 (1962) 229-38.
The assimilated form in Aramaic is Babylonian and not Palestinian;
targumic evidence. Mark drew on Hebrew and Aramaic sources.

305. Rabinowitz, I. "Ephphatha (Mark VII.34): Certainly Hebrew,
Not Aramaic," *JSS* 16 (1971) 151-56.
R. reacts to Emerton and Black. Mark 5:41 is Aramaic, but 7:34
is Hebrew (nip^Cal masc. sg. imv.).

306. Rinaldi, G. "Il Targum palestinese del Pentateuco," *BeO* 17
(1975) 75-77.
A presentation of Vol. IV of the *editio princeps* of Neofiti 1. The
printed text has been established by the editor. The significance
of Neof. Num for 1 Thess 5:19-20; 2 Pet 2:1, 15-16; Rev 20:7-9.

307. Roberts, B. J. *The Old Testament Text and Versions* (Cardiff:
University of Wales, 1951).
The treatment of the Targumim (pp. 197-213) depends largely on the
work of Kahle. Mark 15:34 (Matt 27:46) and Eph 4:8 are recognized
as NT evidence for pre-Christian Tgs. R. also mentions the relation
of messianic concepts in Tg. Neb. to the NT (e.g. Isa 42:1-4 and
Matt 12:18-21; Isa 53).

308. Rubinkiewicz, R. "Ps LXVIII 19 (=Eph IV 8). Another Textual
Tradition or Targum?" *NovT* 17 (1975) 219-24.
A shorter form of the text, applying it to God and not to Moses, can
be traced to the 2nd cent. B. C. In Eph Paul is not interested in
the Moses-Christ typology; Jesus is the true God who ascended into
heaven.

309. Rüger, H. "'Mit welchem Mass ihr messt, wird euch gemessen
werden'," *ZNW* 60 (1969) 174-82.
Various forms of the maxim in targumic and rabbinic literature.
The passive form is closest to Matt 7:2 (cf. Tg. Gen 37:32; 38:25).
Matt 7:2 is not likely the first eschatological use of the saying.

310. Sabourin, L. "The MEMRA of God in the Targums," *BTB* 6 (1976)
79-85.
A summary of Muñoz León's book, *Dios-Palabra*.

311. Sabugal, S. "'...Y la Verdad os hará libres' (Jn 8,32 a la luz
de TP 1 Gen 15,11)," *AugRom* 14 (1975) 177-81.
Except for Neof. Gen 15:11 and Neof. m., Jewish texts concerning
the freedom of Abraham's descendants are relatively late. Liberty
based on the merits of Abraham is seen as a real servitude in
John 8:34.

312. Sánchez Caro, J. M. "Las recensiones targumicas. Estudio de
T. Deut. 1.1," *Salmant* 19 (1972) 605-34.

A genealogical study of the interrelationship of the Tgs. based on
a synoptic study of Tg. Deut 1:1. A subsequent article is to deal
with the passage from Jewish liturgy to Christian anaphora.

313. Schäfer, P. *Die Vorstellung vom heiligen Geist in der
rabbinischen Literatur* (SANT 28; München: Kosel, 1972).
The Tgs. are used, but not in relation to NT texts. Considerable
attention is devoted to the presence of prophecy in Israel and of
the Shekinah during the time of the second temple. The holy spirit
was a national charism which left the first temple and is expected
at the end of time. There is no explicit statement about the holy
spirit passing from the prophets to the rabbis. NT texts are
mentioned.

314. Schäfer, P. "Die Termini 'Heiliger Geist' und 'Geist der
Prophetie' in den Targumim und das Verhältnis der Targumim
zueinander," *VT* 20 (1970) 304-14.
Neof. doesn't use "spirit of prophecy" and its presence in Neof. gl.
is seen as secondary. Onq. uses the formula almost exclusively;
Ps.-J. is mixed; Frg. always uses "holy spirit." "Spirit of
prophecy" is older than the Babylonian Talmud and more biblical.
"Holy spirit" replaced Shekinah, but we know little of the age of
the expression. These terms do not prove that Onq. is more recent
than Pal. Tgs.

315. Schlosser, J. "Les jours de Noé et de Lot. A propos de Luc,
XVII, 26-30," *RB* 80 (1973) 13-36.
The Tgs. introduce the notion of judgment into the Jewish traditions
about Noah and Lot. Evidence for the antiquity of the targumic
traditions. Does Luke 17:26-30 concern the suddenness of eschatological judgment or the certitude of judgment for sinners?

316. Schnackenburg, R. "Zur Herkunft des Johannesevangeliums,"
BZ 14 (1970) 1-23.
S. acknowledges the worthwhile contribution of targumic studies
to the interpretation of the Fourth Gospel (p.3).

317. Schnackenburg, R. *Das Johannesevangelium* II Teil. Kommentar
zu Kap. 5--12 (HTKNT 4; Freiburg/Basel/Wien: Herder, 1971).
Same as above (p.v).

318. Schulz, S. "Die Bedeutung der neuen Targumforschung für die
synoptische Tradition," *Abraham unser Vater* (Festschrift O. Michel;
edd. M. Hengel, P. Schmidt, O. Betz; Leiden/Köln: Brill, 1963)
425-36.

S. discusses Aramaic phrases in the Gospels, such as *rabboun(e)i*,
bar nash. Neof. supports Kahle's position that anti-mishnaic is
pre-mishnaic. On the whole, S. is favorable to the antiquity of
the Pal. Tgs.

319. Serra, A. "Le tradizioni della teofania sinaitica nel Targum
dello pseudo-Jonathan Es. 19.24 e in Giov. 1,19--2,12," *Mar* 33
(1971) 1-39.
A development of suggestions made by Potin. The chronology of
John 1:19--2:12 reflects the chronolgy of the first covenant in
Ps.-J. Exod 19 and 24. Cana is the new Sinai in John as is the
transfiguration in the Synoptics.

320. Serra, A. "Una monografia su Apocalisse 12," *Mar* 38 (1976)
19-28.
Tg. references are added to the study of H. Gollinger, *Das "grosse
Zeichen" von Apokalypse* 12 (SBM 11; Würzburg/Stuttgart: Echter/KBW,
1971), esp. Gen 3:15; Exod 15:12, 18; 24:10.

321. Serra, A. *Contributi dell'Antica Litteratura Guidaica per
l'Esegesi di Giovanni 2:1-12 e 19:25-27* (Scripta Pontificae
Facultatis Theologiae "Marianum" 31; Roma: Herder, 1977).

322. Sidebottom, E. *James, Jude and 2 Peter* (The Century Bible.
New Edition; London: Nelson, 1967).
With reference to Jude 11, Cain is the type of the cynical worldling
in Philo and the Pal. Tg. (p. 30).

323. Snodgrass, K. R. "1 Peter ii.1-10: Its Formation and Literary
Affinities," *NTS* 24 (1977) 97-106.
1 Peter is not dependent on other NT texts, but all are dependent
on pre-Christian Jewish tradition which associated Isa 8:14 and
28:16. Ps 118:22 was added to these stone texts through the
conclusion of the parable of the wicked tenants (Mark 12:1-12 par.)
and early apologetic for the resurrection (Acts 4:11). Cf. Tg.
Isa 8:14; 28:1-21; Jer 51:26; Zech 4:7, 10; Ps 118:22.

324. Speier, S. "'Das Kosten des Todeskelches' im Targum," *VT* 13
(1963) 344.
With reference to Le Déaut's article (*Bib* 1962), *ks' dmwt* is also
attested in Tg. Gen 40:23, as found in Neof., Frg. (Rabbinic Bible
of 1517), 110 (ed. Ginsburger), but not in Ps.-J.

325. Spiegel, S. *The Last Trial. On the Legends and Lore of the
Command to Abraham to Offer Isaac as a Sacrifice: The Akedah*

(Translated from the Hebrew with Introduction by Judah Goldin;
New York: Pantheon, 1967).
In this literary work, the author uses the Tgs., the NT, and other
early Jewish and Christian literature. Goldin's introduction
speaks of the midrashic process.

326. Strobel, A. "Die Passa-Erwartung als urchristliches Problem
in Lc 17:20f.," *ZNW* 49 (1958) 157-96.
Paratērēsis has the theological sense of messianic expectation
associated with Passover night in Pal. Tg. Exod 12:42; it is also
associated with astronomical observations; cf. Gal 4:10. The Lucan
saying rejects this popular effort to calculate the time of the
end.

327. Strobel, A. "A. Merx über Lc 17:20f.," *ZNW* 51 (1960) 133-34.
A citation from A. Merx *Die vier kanonischen Evangelien* II, 2,
1905, p. 345: Luke's text is a rejection of Pharisaic speculation
concerning the coming of the Messiah based on Pal. Tg. Exod 12:42.

328. Strobel, A. *Untersuchungen zum eschatologischen Verzögerungs-
problem auf Grund der spätjüdisch-urchristlichen Geschichte von
Habakuk 2,2ff.* (NovTSup 2; Leiden: Brill, 1961).
Tg. Hab 2:3, Isa 46:13 ($^c kb$) suggest a wider, less linear sense
for *'ḥr* than LXX (*chronizein*).

329. Strobel, A. "In dieser Nacht (Luk 17,34). Zu einer älteren
Form der Erwartung in Luk 17,20-37," *ZTK* 58 (1961) 16-29.
The article deals primarily with the expectation of the end in
1st cent. Judaism. Reference is made to the expectation of
Passover night, but no explicit reference is made to Tgs. in this
connection. Onq., Neof. Exod 17: 7 (*bynn'*) is adduced with
reference to Luke 17:29 (*entos hymōn*).

330. Testa, E. "Il Targum di Is 55,1.13, scoperto a Nazareth, e la
teologia sui pozzi dell acqua viva," *SBFLA* 17 (1967) 259-89.
A fragmentary inscription from Nazareth is reconstructed to contain
a text of Tg. Isa 55:1-13, dating from 70-130 A. D. T. sees here
a Jewish-Christian tradition concerning the saving work of the
Word, issuing from the mouth of Yahweh (or the womb of Mary). The
well tradition in the OT, Judaism, the NT, and the Christian Fathers.

331. Testa, E. "Due frammenti di Targum sull'Incarnazione scoperti
a Nazareth," *TerSa* 43 (1967) 99-104.
See above.

332. Thompson, W. *Matthew's Advice to a Divided Community. Mt. 17,
22--18,35* (AnBib 44; Rome: Pontifical Biblical Institute, 1970).
The targumic formula, $š^e rî\ uš^e baq$, "to loose and to forgive," in
Neof. and Ps.-J. is used (pp. 192-93) to explain the vocabulary
of Matt 16:19; 18:18 (cf. John 20:23).

333. Torrey, C. *Our Translated Gospels* (New York: Harper & Bros.,
1938).
The Tgs. are used sporadically in matters of grammar and vocabulary
to explain mistranslations. There is no Targum index.

334. Tosato, A. *Il Matrimonio nel guidaismo antico e nel Nuovo
Testamento* (Roma: Città Nuova, 1976).
Deals with the treatment of Adam and Eve in the Tgs. (pp. 74-78),
esp. Gen 1:27; 2:24; 5:2; 35:9; Deut 32:4; 34:6); God joined Adam
and Eve in marriage. Cf. Mark 10:9; Matt 19:6.

335. Tuñí, J. *La verdad os hará libres (Jn 8,32). Liberación y
libertad del creyente, en el cuarto evangelio* (Barcelona: Herder,
1973).
The Tgs. show a tendency towards uniformity in rendering texts
concerning the freedom of slaves, and liberation from Egypt. The
use of these and other Jewish traditions in the messianic and
eschatological sense at the feast of Tabernacles and their application to John 8:31-59. There is a Targum index.

336. Urbach, E. *The Sages: Their Concepts and Beliefs* 2 vols.
(Translated from the 2nd Hebrew edition 1971; Jerusalem: Hebrew
University, Magnes Press, 1975).
References to Christianity and the NT are generally rare in this
study. Pp. 30-36 treat of Abraham as the first believer with
reference to Ps.-J. Gen 15:6; 1 Tim 4:1, 6; Tit 1:4; Jas 2:14-26;
Rom 1:5; 10:5, 6; 10; 11:6; 4:16; Gal 3:11; faith in Judaism, Paul,
and Jewish Christianity. There is a Targum index.

337. Van Unnik, W. "'With unveiled face'. An Exegesis of II Cor.
3:12-18," *NovT* 6 (1963) 153-69.
Paul's use of *parrēsia* reflects the Aramaic *glh' pyn* or *glh r's*.
In the Tgs. the expression connotes freedom, not insolence as in
later literature.

338. Vermès, G. "Baptism and Jewish Exegesis: New Light from Ancient
Sources," *NTS* 4 (1958) 308-19.
A sacrificial and expiatory interpretation of the blood of

circumcision is preserved in Tg. Exod 4:24-26, and perhaps in the
LXX. This early tradition may have influenced Paul in Rom 6:3-4
and Col 2:11-12.

339. Vermès, G. *Scripture and Tradition in Judaism. Haggadic
Studies* (SPB 4; Leiden: Brill, 1961; 2nd ed. 1973).
A collection of studies, some published previously, concerning the
origins and development of Jewish haggadic traditions. I: The
Symbolism of Words; II: The Rewritten Bible; III: Balaam; Baptism
and Jewish Exegesis; Redemption. The 2nd ed. is substantially
unchanged, with minor revisions and corrections. See subsequent
entries.

340. Vermès, G. "Redemption and Genesis XXII. The Binding of Isaac
and the Sacrifice of Jesus," *Scripture and Tradition in Judaism*
(2nd ed. 1973) 193-227.
The binding of Isaac is the cornerstone of Jewish theology of the
love of God. The significance of Tg. Gen 22 in Jewish tradition.
The Tamid and Passover particularly are memorials of the Akedah
and Isaac is the prototype of the risen man. Commemorated at
Passover prior to 70 A. D. Significance for NT theology of the
redemption.

341. Vermès, G. "The Story of Balaam. The Scriptural Origin of
Haggadah," *Scripture and Tradition in Judaism* (2nd ed. 1973)
127-77.
A verse by verse examination of Num 22--24 in Jewish tradition,
pre-Christian and rabbinic. The negative evaluation in the Tgs.
and the NT derives from the evaluation of P in Num 31:8, 16;
Josh 13:22.

342. Vermès, G. "The Life of Abraham (1). Haggadic Development:
A Retrogressive Historical Study," *Scripture and Tradition in
Judaism* (2nd ed. 1973) 67-95.
Traditions about the life of Abraham in the 11th cent. *Sefer ha-
Yashar* are traced back to pre-Christian times. Some of these
traditions are of significance for the NT: e.g. the infancy of
Abraham and Matt 2; profit from idolatry and Acts 19:23-27;
miraculous signs and Matt 1:20; Luke 1:26-35; Tg. Exod 1:15; 34:7
and John 1:29. The Tgs. are used frequently.

343. Vermès, G. "The Life of Abraham (2). Haggadic Development:
A Progressive Historical Study," *Scripture and Tradition in
Judaism* (2nd ed. 1973) 96-126.

1QapGen 12:8--15:4 in the light of the OT and Jewish tradition,
including the Tgs. 1QapGen is the lost link between biblical and
rabbinic midrash.

344. Vermès, G. "Lion--Damascus--Meḥoḳeḳ--Man. Symbolic Tradition
in the Dead Sea Scrolls," *Scripture and Tradition in Judaism*
(2nd ed. 1973) 40-66.
Four studies of the symbolism acquired by these terms in the LXX,
Tgs., Qumran, and later Jewish tradition. Qumran confirms the
early date of the messianic interpretation, both royal and
prophetic.

345. Vermès, G. *Jesus the Jew* (London: Collins, 1973).
A Targum index isolates the use made of the Tgs. in this attempt
to draw a historical picture of Jesus against the background of
1st cent. Judaism.

346. Vermès, G. *Post-Biblical Jewish Studies* (SJLA 8; Leiden:
Brill, 1975).
A collection of twelve articles published elsewhere, revised and
updated. Good indices. See subsequent entries. Three are of
special interest to NT scholars.

347. Vermès, G. "The Qumran Interpretation of Scripture in its
Historical Setting," *Post-Biblical Jewish Studies* (1975) 37-49.
In this article the targumic and Qumran interpretations of Num 24:17
and Hab 2:4 are compared. Cf. Matt 2:1-12; Rom 1:17; Gal 3:11;
Heb 10; 38, 39.

348. Vermès, G. "The Use of BAR NASH/BAR NASHA in Jewish Aramaic,"
in M. Black, *An Aramaic Approach to the Gospels and Acts* (3rd ed.
1967) 310-28. Reprinted in *Post-Biblical Jewish Studies* (1975)
147-65.
V. extends the base of Lietzmann's earlier study. This study
defends the use of the formula for the first person singular (cf.
Matt 16:13 and Mark 8:27). He cannot find evidence of its use as a
messianic title. In the latter form of the article, there is a
bibliography of critical reaction to his study and his reply in
Jesus the Jew (1973) 160-91; 256-61.

349. Vermès, G. "'He is the Bread.' Targum Neofiti Exodus 16:15,"
Neotestamentica et Semitica. Studies in Honor of Matthew Black
(Edinburgh: T. & T. Clark, 1969) 256-63. Reprinted in a revised
version in *Post-Biblical Jewish Studies* (1975) 139-46.

The peculiar reading of Neof. Exod 16:15 and Jewish tradition in general suggest a personal interpretation of Moses as the manna. Significance for 1 Cor 10:4; John 6:31-51. But see Le Déaut, *BTB* 4 (1974) 278 n. 110: scribal error in Neof.

350. Vermès, G. "Bible and Midrash: Early Old Testament Exegesis," *Post-Biblical Judaism* (1975) 59-91.
A revision of the article which appeared in *The Cambridge History of the Bible* (Cambridge: University Press, 1970) I 199-231. Bibliography.

351. Vermès, G. "The Targumic Versions of Genesis 4:3-16," ALUOS 3 (Leiden: Brill, 1963) 81-114. In a revised and updated form in *Post-Biblical Jewish Studies* (1975) 92-126.
The doctrinal significance of these texts. Onq. is a revised version of a proto-Ps.-J. or Onq. and Ps.-J. derived from a common Palestinian source. Application to NT texts.

352. Vermès, G. "Ḥanina ben Dosa," *Post-Biblical Jewish Studies* (1975) 178-214.
"Men of truth" and "those who hate evil gain" in Tg. Exod 18:21 and in praise of Ḥanina ben Dosa (*Mek. R. Ishmael* on Exod 18:21) also describe Jesus in the Gospels. His disciples are also called to be such.

353. Wensinck, A. "The Semitisms of Codex Bezae and their Relation to the non-Western Text of the Gospel of Saint Luke," *Bulletin of the Bezan Club* 12 (1937) 11-48.
D frequently, though not always, preserves a reading closer to a semitic source than mss. of the non-Western tradition. Most examples are grammatical or purely verbal, but targumic support is frequently adduced.

354. Wieder, N. *The Judean Scrolls and Karaism* (London: East and West Library, 1962).
Chapter I, "The Land of Damascus," utilizes both the Tgs. and the NT to explain the messianic sense of Galilee, esp. with respect to Matt 4:15-16; the Transfiguration; and Mark 14:28.

355. Wilcox, M. "The Old Testament in Acts 1--15," *AusBR* 5 (1956) 1-41.
The article examines OT citations in the speeches of Acts which differ from the LXX. They are frequently similar to the Tgs., but do not reproduce all the same detail. Dependence is indirect and through a Greek source.

356. Wilcox, M. *The Semitisms of Acts* (Oxford: Clarendon, 1965).
Evidence for semitic sources in Acts 1--15; 22; 26. Targumic
textual traditions in Acts 7; 13 and elsewhere. See subject index.
Aramaic and targumic influence may be indirect through the Greek.
Pal. Tgs. are important for the study of the NT.

357. Wilcox, M. "The Judas-Tradition in Acts I.15-26," *NTS* 19
(1973) 438-52.
The material in vv 15b, 17, 18, 19b is pre-Lucan. Pal. Tg. Gen
44:18 (CTg.D) is the source of the Scripture quotation in v 17.
The present text is Luke's attempt to understand his Greek source.
The concept of the Twelve is pre-Lucan.

358. Wilcox, M. "Peter and the Rock: A Fresh Look at Matthew
XVI.17-19," *NTS* 22 (1976) 78-33.
Tg. Ps 118:22 interprets *'eben* of the young man or child (*ṭalyā*)
forsaken by the "builders," i.e. the scholars, but who becomes the
Messiah, the son of Jesse. Reflections of this interpretation in
the NT "stone-rock"-texts, esp. Matt 16:17-19.

359. Wilcox, M. "'Upon the Tree'--Deut 21:22-23 in the New
Testament," *JBL* 96 (1977) 85-99.
The Tgs., Qumran and rabbinic literature show that Deut 21:22-23
were a subject of debate from earliest times. The use of this
text and the "tree" motif in the NT (cf. Gal 3:13; Acts 5:30; 10:39;
13:29; John 19:31) reflect this debate and fostered the application
of the figure of Isaac to Jesus.

360. Wood, E. "Isaac Typology in the New Testament," *NTS* 14 (1968)
583-89.
A review of scholarly literature on the influence of Jewish traditions concerning Isaac and the Akedah on the NT and early Christian
writers.

361. Wright, A. "The Literary Genre Midrash," *CBQ* 28 (1966) 105-38;
417-57. Published in book form with minor improvements as *The
Literary Genre Midrash* (Staten Island: Alba House, 1968).
In an attempt to clarify the use of the term "midrash" with
reference to the NT, W. defines it in terms of the later rabbinic
literary genre, closely related to the biblical text which it
interprets for a new set of circumstances.

362. York, A. "The Dating of the Targumic Literature," *JSJ* 5
(1974) 49-62.

A critical evaluation of the arguments for an early dating of the
Pal. Tgs. of the Pentateuch.   Y. nonetheless acknowledges the
antiquity of traditions, early written targums, and their importance
for NT study.   His cautions concern the dating of extant texts.

(The first number refers to the pertinent item in the annotated
bibliography; the numbers following the comma refer to the pertinent
pages.)

Matt 1--2
Targumic traditions, especially concerning Moses. 145; 301; 6.

Matt 1:3
Tamar in early Jewish tradition; see Pal. Tg. Gen 38:1-30. 138,
156; 96; 234,51; 245,48.

Matt 1:18-23
See 1QapGen 2:1-2, 19-23; 5:3-25. 171,399-400.

Matt 2
Influence of targumic traditions concerning Moses, Abraham, the
return to Israel, Laban and Balaam; contact with Tgs. in citations;
see Ps.-J. Exod 1:15; Num 22:5; Tg. Isa 41:2-3; Num 24:7. 7,212-23;
138,157-58; 6; 41; 342; 296,156-58.163; 171,399-400; 22,54; 275;
119,189-92.

Matt 2:2
Messianic character of Tg. Num 24:17. 362,55; 138,160-62; 296,
106-15; 86,367-68; 344,59; 341,165-66; 347,48.

Matt 2:5-6
Neof. m. Gen 35:19; 48:7; Bethlehem of Juda as Rachel's burial
place; messianic sense of Tg. Mic 5:1, 3; cf: also Ps.-J. Gen 35:21.
138,183; 123; 34,99-101; 362,55; 200,91; 87,299; 284,52-53; 86,368.

Matt 2:13-18
Laban identified with Balaam (Frg. Num 22:5) and influence of
Jewish legend on Matt. 120.

Matt 2:14
Cf. Ps.-J. Gen 47:14 (?). 238,20.

Matt 2:15
See Tg. Exod 4:22; Hos 11:1; Gen 1:1. 241,28; 87,299; 119,191.

Matt 2:18
See Tg. Jer 31:15. 34,102-03.

Matt 2:23
Nētser is interpreted messianically in Tg. Isa 11:1.   187,240-41;
141,201; 200,104; 34,103-04.

Matt 3:1-5
New exodus evoked at beginning of Jesus' ministry.   230,310-11.

Matt 3:2 etc.
"Kingdom of heaven" out of reverence for name of God; a targumism.
141,202.

Matt 3:7
Ps.-J. Gen 4:1-2 an early tradition.   182.

Matt 3:9
Play on *bn* and *'bn*; cf. Onq. Gen 49:24.   Abraham as the father of
proselytizers; cf. Neof. Gen 12:1-5.   238,28-29; 212,374-76; 124,
106-07; 279,142-43.

Matt 3:10
Karpon poiein, a Hebrew and Aramaic idiom; cf. Tg. Gen 1:11, 12;
Jer 17:8.   92,138-39.

Matt 3:13-17
Literary form based on Pal. Tg. Gen 22:10; 28:12 (Deute-vision).
Dove and the congregation of Israel; cf. Tg. Ps 68:14.   Cf. also
Tg. Gen 3:22-23.   251,195-248; 141,204; 119,31.

Matt 3:17
Ho agapētos: ḥbyb; cf. Tg. Ps 2:7; Isa 42:1 etc.   Isaac typology.
Divine pleasure and targumic usage.   *Bath qol* and the Tgs.   200,
29-32; 263,30-33; 27; 24,323-24; 118,68-71; 272,96-97.113-14.

Matt 4:1-11
Temptation narrative and Jewish interpretation of Deut 6:5; cf.
Ps.-J.,Onq.   179.

Matt 4:4
See Tg. Deut 8:3.   200,66-69.

Matt 4:16
On theme of liberation, cf. Tg. Isa 8:23--9:1; Pss 18:29; 132:17.
241,29; 87,307-09; 354,25-30.

Matt 5:5
Tēn gēn reflects Tg. Ps 37:11.   200,133.

Matt 5:8
"Pure of heart"; cf. Tg. Lev 9:6.   234,49.

Matt 5:12
Haggadic tradition of Abraham's reward in Tg. Gen 15:1; other
references to "reward" in Pal. Tg. 272,131-32.

Matt 5:21
See Onq., Ps.-J. Gen 9:6. 267,126-31.

Matt 5:22
Inextinguishable fire; Neof. Gen 3:24; 28:25; 39:9; Neof. m. 49:22.
138,178-79; 303,231; 284,69-71; 272,136-37.

Matt 5:23-24
Making peace with the wronged; see Ps.-J. Lev 6:5-6; Deut 22:4.
127,111; 234,68.

Matt 5:29-30
Gehenna; cf. Frg. Gen 38:25. 267,141.

Matt 5:38
Ps.-J. Lev 24:20 reflects rabbinic modification; Onq. and Neof.
literal. 267,131.

Matt 5:43
Ps.-J. Lev 19:18 glosses the text differently. 32.

Matt 5:48
267,133-38; 235,53; 92,181; 155; 200,73-74; 14; 166,196.

Matt 6:1, 4
"Reward" in the Pal. Tg. 272,131-32.

Matt 6:15
En tais goniais tōn plateiōn; cf. Tg. Prv 7:12. 92,177.

Matt 6:6, 8
"Your Father who is in heaven"; cf. Ps.-J. Exod 1:19; Frg. Num
21:9; Gen 21:33. 272,116-17.

Matt 6:9-13
Expressions common to Tgs. and the Lord's prayer; e.g. Neof.
Exod 32:31; Gen 18:20-26. 92,298; 141,209; 215.

Matt 6:9
Formula "Father who is in heaven" in Tgs.; e.g. Neof. Exod 1:19;
Num 20:21; Deut 33:24 etc. 141,207; 272,115-19.

Matt 6:11
On *epiousios*, cf. Tgs. for similar expressions. 92,203-07; 236,
391-92; 200,74-75.

Matt 6:12
Debt for sin; cf. Neof. Exod 32:31; Gen 18:20-26. 141,209; 272,120.

Matt 6:19-20
Heavenly treasures; cf. Tg. Gen 15:1.   279,129.

Matt 6:24
For *mamōnas*, see CTg.C Gen 34:23.   92,139-40; 236,391; 172,90.

Matt 7:2
Examples from Tgs.; e.g. Tg. Gen 38:26; Lev 26:43; Frg., Neof.
Num 12:15; Ps.-J. Num 12:14; Tg. Isa 27:8.   248,246; 256,141; 309;
144,108; 267,138-42; 249a,I 353.

Matt 7:5
See Frg. Gen 49:22.   92,303.

Matt 7:6
Play on words, *qdš* = "ring" in 11QtgJob 38:8.   172,95.

Matt 7:12
Altruistic love in Judaism and Christianity; cf. Ps.-J. Lev 19:18,
34.   174.

Matt 7:17-19
Karpon poiein a Hebrew and Aramaic idiom; cf. Tg. Gen 1:11, 12;
Jer 17:8.   92,138-39; 236,391.

Matt 7:21
See Frg., Neof. Num 20:21.   272,119.

Matt 8:22
Possible word play with Aramaic *mtn* - "to delay, put off a
decision": "Let the waverers (*mtnyyn*) bury their dead (*mytyhwn*)";
cf. Pal. Tg. Lev 24:12; Num 9:8; 15:34.   92,207-08.

Matt 9:4
"To think in the heart"; cf. Neof. Num 21:5.   86,368.

Matt 9:12
Bari' = "strong and healthy"; cf. Tg. Exod 4:7.   92,196.

Matt 9:13
H reflects targumic reading of Hos 6:6.   24,321.

Matt 9:20
Kraspedon also in Onq. Num 15:38.   21,465.

Matt 10:6
Cf. Tg. Jer 50:6.   200,135.

Matt 10:32-33
Reverential manner of speaking of God reflects targumic practice.
272,93-95.

Matt 10:40
Play on Aramaic *qbl*; cf. Tg. Deut 18:18-19.   86,371; 99,376-78.

Matt 11:10
Geber in Jewish tradition and John the Baptist.   344,56-66.

Matt 11:11
See Frg. Exod 14:29; Pal. Tg. Num 23:10.   92,298; 234,50.

Matt 11:12
See Tg. Exod 19:21-24 and LXX.   119,292.288.

Matt 11:19
See Ps.-J., Pal. Tg., Onq. Deut 21:20.   187,126; 200,80-81.

Matt 11:26
Targumic manner of expression.   272,95-96.

Matt 11:28-30
See Tg. Esth II 8:13; Pal. Tg. Deut 25:18.   92,183-84; 286,494-95.

Matt 12:4
Showbread; cf. Onq., Ps.-J. Exod 25:30.   213,58 (ET:64).

Matt 12:7
H reflects targumic reading of Hos 6:6.   24,321.

Matt 12:18-21
Cf. Tg. Isa 42:1-4.   200,110-16; 263,30-33; 34,107-15.

Matt 12:28
"Kingdom come upon them"; cf. Tg. Ezek 7:2-10.   80,230.

Matt 12:40
Resurrection "on the third day" or "after three days"; cf. Tg.
Hos 6:2. Jonah as a figure of Christ.   266; 234,45.

Matt 12:50
See Frg., Neof. Num 20:21.   272,119.

Matt 13
Tgs. and setting of seed parables; cf. Tg. Jer 4:3; Hos 10:21;
Ezek 17:22-24.   110.

Matt 13:1-9, 18-23
The parable of the sower and the Shema (Deut 6:5) in Jewish
exegesis.   180.

Matt 13:16-17
See Neof. Gen 49:18; also Tg. Isa 52:13-15; 35:5; Pal. Tg. Num
24:3, 4, 15; Gen 49:1.   138,173; 267,243-45; 112,307; 284,53;
198; 286,463; 272,139-40.

Matt 13:26
Karpon poiein a Hebrew and Aramaic idiom; cf. Tg. Gen 1:11, 12;
Jer 17:8.   92,138-39.

Matt 14:36
Kraspedon also in Onq. Num 15:38.   21,465.

Matt 15:5
Contemporary evidence for the use of *qorban*.   172,89-90.

Matt 15:24
Cf. Tg. Jer 50:6.   200,135.

Matt 15:26
Neof. Exod 22:30.   248,247; 138,184.

Matt 16:13
Son of Man as circumlocution; targumic evidence.   348,163.

Matt 16:16
Pal. Tg. Gen 49:10-12 and messianism.   138,167-69; 195,22-32.

Matt 16:17-19
Tg. Ps 118:22 and play on *'bn, bn*; also *ṭly'*; cf. other NT stone
texts.   358; 212,374-76.

Matt 16:19
Targumic use of *šry, šbq, nṭr*.   Keys in Frg. P V, Neof. Gen 30:22;
Ps.-J. Deut 28:12.   235,177-78; 248,246; 351,95.102.121-24; 86,368;
163; 332,192-93; 135,231; 138,163; 272,129-30; 350,65; 238,17.

Matt 16:21
See Tg. Hos 6:1-2.   95,5-7.

Matt 17:1-9
Targumic references to cloud of glory, revelation of the kingdom
of God, high mountain.   Fourth night in Pal. Tg. Exod 12:42.
Tabernacles in Judaism and the Tgs.   256,212-20; 354,15-17; 286,
329; 28.

Matt 17:4
Cloud of glory and presence of God; Ps.-J. Exod 13:20; Onq.,
Ps.-J. Lev 23:42.   232,89-90.

Matt 17:5
Ho agapētos: ḥbyb; Tg. Ps 2:7 etc.   Isaac typology probable.
Divine pleasure and targumic usage.   *Bath qol* and Tgs.   Overshadowing cloud and Tgs.   200,36-37; 263,30-33; 118,68-71; 272,
96-97; 272,113-14; 119,27-36.

Matt 17:22-23
See Tg. Hos 6:1-2.   95,5-7.

Matt 18:3
Evidence from Neof. for *ḥzr* = *strephein*.   236,390-91.

Matt 18:8-9
Inextinguishable fire; Neof. Gen 38:25; 39:9; Neof. m. Gen 49:22.
138,178-79; 303,231; 272,136-37; 267,141.

Matt 18:14
Targumic manner of expression.   272,95-96.

Matt 18:18
Targumic use of *šry*, *šbq*, *nṭr*.   235,177-78; 248,246; 138,163-64;
351,95.102.121-24; 86,368; 163; 332,192-93; 272,129-30; 135,231;
350,65.

Matt 18:20
Presence of God in every prayer assembly; Frg. Exod 20:21.   350,84.

Matt 18:22
Lamech's pardon in Pal. Tg. Gen 4:24.   138,182-83.

Matt 19:5-6
God as the author of marriage in Ps.-J. Deut 34:6; Gen 35:8; Pal.
Tg. Deut 32:4; Frg. Gen 1:27.   248,250-51; 127,385; 334,74-78;
119,81.368.

Matt 19:10
Aitia and Tg. Gen 2:21-22 (?).   119,85.

Matt 19:16-30
The Shema in the Tgs.   272,125.

Matt 19:17-19
The Decalogue in the Targums.   150.

Matt 19:28
Paliggenesia and eschatological renewal in Jewish tradition.   230,
252-55.

Matt 20:18-19
See Tg. Hos 6:1-2.   95,5-7.

Matt 20:22-23
Pal. Tg. Gen 40:23; Deut 32:1.   248,246; 138,166; 226; 324; 92,298;
234,47.

Matt 21:1-9
See Onq. Gen 49.   82,21.

Matt 21:5
Tg. Zech 9:9 messianic.   87,299-300; 28,96.

Matt 21:9
Tg. Gen 49:10-12 and messianism.   Messianic character of Tg.
Ps 118:23-29.   213,249 (ET:259).

Matt 21:13
Tg. Isa 56:1-9; 57:19 reflect Exod 21:1--22:23--*seder* and *haptara*.
Influence of synagogue readings.   299.

Matt 21:33-46
Word play on '*bn*, *bn* in Tg. Ps 118:22.   358; 212,374-76; 95,11-14.

Matt 22:1-14
Targumic references to war, feasting and the Messiah; esp. Ps.-J.
Deut 20:10-12.   127,127-36.

Matt 22:13
Eschatological symbolism of light and darkness; cf. Pal. Tg. Exod
12:42.   230,256.

Matt 22:15-22
Resurrection of the dead; cf. Neof. Gen 19:26 etc.   138,176-77.

Matt 23:5
Kraspedon also in Onq. Num 15:38.   21,465.

Matt 23:8-10
Tg. 2 Kgs 2:12 changes "my father" to "my rabbi"; cf. Tg. 2 Kgs
13:14.   119,25.

Matt 23:15
Flames of hell; cf. Neof. Num 21:21; 31:50.   86,368-69.

Matt 23:16
See Tg. Esth II 1:9.   92,252.

Matt 23:35
Tg.Lam 2:20 and the identification of Zechariah; portrayal of
Cain and Abel.   248,248; 138,164; 200,86-88; 4; 267,156-63; 351;
224,30-36.

Matt 23:39
Messianic character of Tg. Ps 118:23-29.   213,249 (ET:259).

Matt 24:3
See Pal. Tg. Exod 12:42.   256,202.

Matt 24:7
See Neof. Num 24:23.   284,64.

Matt 24:24
See Neof., Ps.-J. Deut 13:1-3. 200,50-51; 40,163; 234,46.

Matt 24:29-31
Theophany of Sinai in Tgs. 303,242-43.

Matt 24:32-33
Play on *qyṣ* and messianic reference in Pal. Tg. Gen 49:1; Tg.
Jer 8:20. 297; 245,45-56.

Matt 24:51
See Tg. Isa 53:12 for construction. 92,256-57.

Matt 25:6
Messiah comes at night; cf. Pal. Tg. Exod 12:42. 256,202.

Matt 25:31, 34, 40
Pal. Tg. Num 11:26. 284,58-59.

Matt 25:41
Vision of Gehenna in Pal. Tg. Gen 15:17; Gen 3:24. Flames of hell;
cf. Neof. Num 21:21; 31:50. 284,73-75; 272,136-37; 86,368-69.

Matt 25:35-45
Works of charity and Pal. Tg. 249a,I 326.

Matt 26:17
First day of unleavened bread; cf. Ps.-J. Lev 23:11; Num 28:18.
213,11 (ET:17).

Matt 26:26
Artos = leavened or unleavened bread; Tgs. Exod 29:2; Lev 8:26 etc.
213,57-59 (ET:63-65).

Matt 26:26-30
Expiation by sprinkling of blood; cf. Tgs. Exod 24:8. 238,23; 234,
35.

Matt 26:27-28
Pal. Tg. Gen 40:23; Deut 32:1. 248,246.

Matt 26:28
Expiatory character of the blood of the covenant in Onq., Ps.-J.
Exod 24:8; "to taste the cup of death"; cf. Neof. Deut 32:1.
Rendering of *polloi* in Tg. Isa 52:14; 53:11-12b. Aramaic character
of formula *to haima mou tes diathēkēs*. 248,252; 200,57-59; 303,152;
226; 325; 213,217 (ET:225-26).219 (ET:227); 141,209-10; 272,127-28.

Matt 26:31
Combination of Zech 13:7 and Isa 53:6 in Tg. Isa 53:6; cf. Tg.
Zech 13:7. 19,81-82; 87,300.

Matt 26:39
Pal. Tg. Gen 40:23; Deut 32:1.   248,246.

Matt 26:52
See Tg. Isa 50:11.   187,126-28; 86,369; 221; 200,144.

Matt 26:63
Pal. Tg. Gen 49:10-12 and messianism.   138,167-69; 195,22-32; 144,
67-69.

Matt 26:64
Tgs. and Torrey on mistranslation.   14.

Matt 26:65-66
Blasphemy according to Lev 24:15 and Tg. Deut 21:23.   127,454-55.

Matt 26:67-68
Messiah to prophesy by smell; cf. Tg. Isa 11:3.   127,408.

Matt 27:9-10
See Tg. Zech 11:13.   87,300.

Matt 27:43
See Tg. Ps 22:9.   33,140-41.

Matt 27:45
Night precedes salvation events.   230,257.

Matt 27:46
See Tg. Ps 22:2.   362,56; 21,177-78; 200,63-66; 222,496-97; 34,
83-87.

Matt 27:48
Spongos also in Onq. Exod 29:23.   21,465.

Matt 27:52
Resurrection of the dead and the appearance of the Messiah
associated with Akedah.   230,206.

Matt 28:20
See Pal. Tg. Exod 12:42.   256,202.

Mark 1:1-5
New exodus evoked at beginning of Jesus's ministry.   230,310-11.

Mark 1:2
Geber in Jewish tradition and John the Baptist.   344,56-66.

Mark 1:9-11
Literary form based on Pal. Tg. Gen 22:10; 28:12--Deute-vision;
cf. also Tg. Gen 3:22-23.   Dove and the congregation of Israel; cf.
Tg. Ps 68:14.   251,195-248; 141,204; 119,31.

Mark 1:11
Ho agapētos: ḥbyb; cf. Tg. Ps 2:7; Isa 42:1.   Isaac typology
probable.   Divine pleasure and targumic usage.   *Bath qol* and Tgs.
200,29-32; 263,30-33; 27; 24,323-24; 118,68-71; 230,203-04; 272,
96-97.113-14.

Mark 1:15
See Tgs. for sense of *ēggiken*; e.g. Tg. Gen 11:14; Job 20:6;
Ps.-J. Gen 37:41.   92,208-11.

Mark 1:27
"New teaching" and Tg. Isa 12:3; 2:3; 32:6; Cant 5:10.   15,70-73;
119,214-15.

Mark 2:4
Ochlos a mistranslation for *špw*[c]: "width."   119,384-85.

Mark 2:17
Bari' - "strong and healthy"; cf. Tg. Exod 4:7.   92,196.

Mark 2:26
Showbread; cf. Onq., Ps.-J. Exod 25:30.   213,58 (ET:64).

Mark 2:28
Generic use of Son of Man; targumic evidence; e.g. Pal. Tg. Gen
4:14.   92,23; 86,363-64; 90,663; 135,223.

Mark 4:1-9, 13-20
The parable of the sower and the Shema (Deut 6:5) in Jewish
exegesis.   180.

Mark 4:12
Citation of Isa 6:9-10 agrees with Tg. rather than MT or LXX; cf.
also Tg. Isa 53:4-5; 57:18.   92,211-16.275-76; 200,33-35; 19,78-81;
24,315; 34,130-31.144.

Mark 4:22
'l' rendered as *alla* or *ei me*; cf. Frg., Neof. Gen 22:14.   92,
113-14.

Mark 4:24
Examples from Tgs.: e.g. Tg. Gen 38:26; Lev 26:43; Tg. Isa 27:8 etc.
248,246; 309; 144,108; 267,138-42.

Mark 4:29
Karpon didonai; cf. Tg. Lev 26:4; 19:23, 24, 25; Joel 4:13.   236,
393; 34,144; 92,164.

Mark 4:32
Poiein karpous; cf. Onq- Gen 49:15, 21.   92,302; 237,391.

Mark 6:56
Kraspedon also in Onq. Num 15:38.   21,465.

Mark 7:11
Contemporary evidence for use of *qorban*.   172,89-90.

Mark 7:27
"Dogs" for pagans in Neof. Exod 22:30.   138,184.

Mark 7:34
Evidence for *ephphatha* as Aramaic or Hebrew.   94; 304; 143; 305.

Mark 8:27
Son of Man as circumlocution; targumic evidence.   348,163.

Mark 8:29
Pal. Tg. Gen 49:10-12 and messianism.   138,167-69; 195,22-32.

Mark 8:31
See Tg. Hos 6:1-2.   95,5-7.

Mark 9:2-10
Targumic references to cloud of glory, revelation of the kingdom
of God, high mountain.   Fourth night in Pal. Tg. Exod 12:42.
Tabernacles in Judaism and Tgs.   256,212-20; 354,15-17; 286,329;
28.

Mark 9:2
Synoptic variant and Aramaic; cf. CTg. Gen 4:5.   16,73.

Mark 9:5
Cloud of glory and presence of God; Ps.-J. Exod 13:20; Onq.,
Ps.-J. Lev 23:42.   232,89-90.

Mark 9:7
Ho agapētos: ḥbyb; Tg. Ps 2:7. Isaac typology probable. *Bath qol*
and Tgs. Overshadowing cloud and Tgs.   200,36-37; 263,30-33; 118,
68-71; 272,113-14; 119,27-36.

Mark 9:31
See Tg. Hos 6:1-2.   95,5-7.

Mark 9:33-37
Tg. evidence for *ṭalya* = "child" or servant."   236,393-94.

Mark 9:43-48
Inextinguishable fire of Gehenna; cf. Frg. Gen 38:25.   267,141.

Mark 9:43
Same use of *kalon--sappir* in Tg. Ruth 2:22.   21,237-38.

Mark 10:6
Targums and Torrey on mistranslation.   14.

Mark 10:6-9

God instituted marriage; see Ps.-J. Deut 34:6; Gen 35:8, and other
targumic evidence.   127,385; 334,74-78; 119,81.368.

Mark 10:15

Tg. evidence for *ṭalya'* = "child" or servant."   236,393-94.

Mark 10:17-31

The Shema in the Tgs.   272,125.

Mark 10:17-19

The Decalogue in the Tgs.   150.

Mark 10:33-34

See Tg. Hos 6:1-2.   95,5-7.

Mark 10:38-39

"To taste the cup of death"; cf. Frg. Gen 40:23; Neof. Deut 32:1.
3; 226; 325.

Mark 10:51

Rabbouni, rabbounei in the Pal. Tg.   92,23-24.44-46; 318,432-33;
86,363; 22,91; 135,231; 234,47; 216.

Mark 11:10

Tg. Gen 49:10-12 and messianism.   Messianic character of Tg. Ps
118:23-29.   82,21; 195,22-32; 213,249 (ET:259).

Mark 12:1-12

Word play on *'bn, bn* in Tg. Ps 118:22.   358; 212,374-76; 95,11-14.

Mark 12:17-27

Resurrection of the dead; cf. Neof. Gen 19:26 etc.   138,176-77.

Mark 12:33

See Onq. Deut 6:4-5.   127,224; 272,123-24.

Mark 12:38

Stolē also in Onq.   21,465.

Mark 13:22

See Neof., Ps.-J. Deut 13:1-3.   200,50-51; 24,315; 34,145; 40,163;
234,46.

Mark 13:24-27
Theophany of Sinai in Tgs.   303,242-43.

Mark 13:26

Son of Man messianic.   138,170; 195,22-32.

Mark 13:28-29

Word play on *qyṣ*; cf. Tg. Jer 8:20.   248,247-48; 297; 245,45-46.

Mark 14:6
See Tg. Gen 31:43. 92,301.

Mark 14:12
First day of unleavened bread; cf. Ps.-J. Lev 23:11; Num 28:18.
213,11 (ET:17).

Mark 14:22
Artos = both leavened and unleavened bread; Tg. Exod 29:2; Lev
8:26 etc. 213,57-59 (ET:63-65).

Mark 14:24
Tgs. attest Aramaic character of formula *to haima mou tēs diathēkēs*.
248,251-52; 141,209-10; 200,57-59; 164; 272,127-28; 213,219
(ET:227); 234,35.

Mark 14:25
Contrast Tg. Cant 8:2: old wine at the messianic banquet. Coming
of the Messiah and Passover night; Frg., Neof. Exod 12:42. 92,
235-56; 189,77-78.

Mark 14:27
For combination of Zech 13:7 and Isa 53:6, see Tg. Isa 53:6. 19,
81-82.

Mark 14:28
"To go before" and messianism; cf. Frg. Exod 12:42; Tg. Ezek 16:12.
354,44-48.

Mark 14:36
See Frg. Gen 40:32: "To taste the cup of death." 92,298; 3.

Mark 14:41
Apechei: Aramaic *dḥyq* and *rḥyq*; examples from Neof. Exod 22:24;
3:9; 5:13. 236,392; 92,225-26.

Mark 14:62
Son of Man messianic. 138,169-70; 195,22-32.

Mark 14:64
Blasphemy according to Lev 24:15 and Tg. Deut 21:23. 127,454-55.

Mark 14:65
Messiah to prophesy by smell; cf. Tg. Isa 11:3. 127,408.

Mark 15:33
Night precedes salvation events. 230,257.

Mark 15:34
Aramaic or Hebrew; cf. Tg. Ps 22:2. 21,177-78; 200,63-66; 24,326-28
222,496-97; 356,53; 34,83-87.

Mark 16:19
Ascension and cloud symbolism. 256,220-25.

Luke 1--2
Use of targumic traditions. Evidence of Palestinian culture.
Expectation of redemption in Pal. Tgs. 145; 43; 301; 272,137-39.

Luke 1:5
Tgs. and Palestinian culture. 43.

Luke 1:8
Taxis in Onq. Num 2:2, 3, 17. 21,465.

Luke 1:9-10
Tgs. and Palestinian culture. 43.

Luke 1:15-16
Geber in Jewish tradition and John the Baptist. 344,56-66.

Luke 1:17, 76
Geber in Jewish tradition and John the Baptist. 344,56-66.

Luke 1:19
Tgs. and Palestinian culture. 43.

Luke 1:32
Pal. Tg. Gen 49:10-12 and messianism. Tg. 2 Sam 7:12-14; 1 Chr
17:10. 138,167-69; 195,22-32; 80,237.

Luke 1:35-38
Overshadowing cloud and Tgs. 119,27-36.

Luke 1:35
Mary as Daughter of Sion; cf. Tg. Zeph 3:14-17. 233.

Luke 1:41, 67
Spirit of prophecy in Pal. Tgs. 272,113.

Luke 1:46-55
Liberation from Egypt background for Magnificat. 230,310; 231,216.

Luke 1:51
See Tg. Isa 51:20. 92,152.

Luke 1:53
See Tg. Ps 107:9; Job 30:10. 92,152.

Luke 1:58
Tgs. and Palestinian culture. 43.

Luke 1:68-79
Background of Exodus and messianic expectation. 230,309.

Luke 2:1-14
Manifestation of the Messiah and Tg. Mic 4:7-10; Ps.-J. Gen 35:21.
223,87; 230,277.

Luke 2:4-18
Messianism and Ps.-J. Gen 35:21.   44.

Luke 2:7
See Tg. Exod 4:22; Hos 11:1; Gen 1:1.   241,28.

Luke 2:8
Tgs. and Palestinian culture.   43.

Luke 2:14
The influence of Tg. Isa 6:3 on the angelic hymn; also influence
of Pal. Tgs. and Jewish liturgy.   248,248; 236,390; 173; 267,204;
92,168; 18,176.

Luke 2:25-32
See Tg. Isa 52:13-15; 35:5; Pal. Tg. Num 24:3, 4, 15.   Fixed time
of redemption; cf. Neof. Gen 49:1.   198; 249a,I 433.

Luke 2:25-27
Spirit of prophecy in Pal. Tgs.   272,113.

Luke 2:25
See Neof. Gen 49:18 etc.   138,173; 267,243; 230,233; 248,286-87;
272,139-40; 92,308.

Luke 2:32
Light, baptism, new creation and Tg. Exod 12:42.   230,256.

Luke 2:37
Tgs. and Palestinian culture.   43.

Luke 2:49
See Frg. Exod 15:2 for "our Father" applied to God by children.
40; 223,141-46.

Luke 3:1-6
New exodus evoked at beginning of Jesus' ministry.   230,310-11.

Luke 3:8
Play on *bn* and *'bn*; cf. Onq. Gen 49:24.   238,28-29; 212,374-76;
245,48.

Luke 3:9
Karpon poiein a Hebrew and Aramaic idiom; cf. Tg. Gen 1:11, 12;
Jer 17:8.   92,138-39.

Luke 3:21-22
Literary form based on Pal. Tg. Gen 22:10; 28:12--Deute-vision;
cf. also Tg. Gen 3:22-23. Dove and the congregation of Israel.
251,195-248; 141,204; 119,31.

Luke 3:22
Ho agapētos: ḥbyb; cf. Tg. Ps 2:7; Isa 42:1 etc. Isaac typology
probable. Divine pleasure and targumic usage. *Bath qol* and Tgs.
200,29-32; 263,30-33; 27; 24,323-24; 118,68-71; 272,96-97.113-14.

Luke 3:38
Divine filiation in Tg. Gen 5:3. 234,59.

Luke 4:1-13
Temptation narrative and Jewish interpretation of Deut 6:5; cf.
Ps.-J., Onq. 179.

Luke 4:4
See Tgs. Deut 8:3. 200,66-69.

Luke 4:16-30
Synagogue readings, homilies, Tgs. and mutual associations. 267,
42-43; 302; 251,146-52; 34,95-96.

Luke 5:19
Ochlos a mistranslation for *špw'':* "width." 119,384-85.

Luke 5:31
Bari' ≠ "strong and healthy"; cf. Tg. Exod 4:7. 92,196.

Luke 6:4
Showbread; cf. Onq., Ps.-J. Exod 25:30. 213,58 (ET:64).

Luke 6:5
Aramaic word plays with *ᶜbd* and *'rwr;* cf. Tg. 2 Kgs 9:34. 92,172.
206.

Luke 6:22
Ekbalōsin to onoma hymōn; cf. Tg. Prv 10:18; Num 13:32; Ps.-J.
Gen 34:30. 92,135-36.

Luke 6:23
See haggadic tradition of Abraham's reward in Tg. Gen 15:1. 200,72.

Luke 6:36
Ps.-J. Lev 22:27-28. 267,133-38; 235,53; 248,246; 92,181; 141,207;
155; 200,73-74; 238,10; 286,286; 14; 166,196; 234,47; 272,118-19;
246,521.

Luke 6:38
Examples from Tgs.: e.g. Tg. Gen 38:26; Lev 26:43; Frg., Neof. Num
12:15; Ps.-J. Num 12:14 etc.   248,246; 256,141; 309; 144,108; 267,
138-42.

Luke 6:42
See Frg. Gen 49:22.   92,303.

Luke 6:43
Karpon poiein a Hebrew and Aramaic idiom; cf. Tg. Gen 1:11, 12;
Jer 17:8.   92,138-39; 236,391.

Luke 7:27
Geber in Jewish tradition and John the Baptist.   Targumism in the
use of Mal 3:1.   344,56-66; 237,44.

Luke 7:28
See Frg. Exod 14:29.   92,298.

Luke 7:34
See Onq., Ps.-J. Deut 21:20.   200,80-81.

Luke 8:4-8, 11-15
The parable of the sower and the Shema (Deut 6:5) in Jewish
exegesis.   180.

Luke 8:8
Karpon poiein a Hebrew and Aramaic idiom; cf. Tg. Gen 1:11, 12;
Jer 17:8.   92,138-39; 236,391.

Luke 8:20
Tg. Gen 49:10-12 and messianism.   195,22-32.

Luke 8:44
Kraspedon also in Onq. Num 15:38.   21,465.

Luke 9:18
Son of Man as circumlocution; targumic evidence.   348,163.

Luke 9:20
Pal. Tg. Gen 49:10-12 and messianism.   138,167-69.

Luke 9:22
See Tg. Hos 6:1-2.   95,5-7.

Luke 9:26
See Pal. Tg. Gen 38:26.   272,135-36.

Luke 9:28-36
Targumic references to cloud of glory, revelation of the kingdom of
God, high mountain.   Fourth night in Pal. Tg. Exod 12:42.   Taber-
nacles in Judaism and Tgs.   256,212-20; 354,15-17; 286,329; 28.

Luke 9:29
Change of countenance and 1QapGen 2:12 and Tg. Gen 4:5, 6.   248,
248-49; 16,73.

Luke 9:31-33
Cloud of glory and presence of God; Ps.-J. Exod 13:20; Onq., Ps.-J.
Lev 23:42.   232,89-90; 119,27-36.

Luke 9:35
Ho agapētos: ḥbyb Tg. Ps 2:7 etc.   Isaac typology.   *Bath qol* and
Tgs.   200,36-37; 263,30-33; 118,68-71; 272,113-14.

Luke 9:60
Possible word play with Aramaic *mtn* = to delay, put off a decision.
"Let the waverers (*mtnyyn*) bury their dead (*mytyhwn*)"; cf. Pal.
Tg. Lev 24:12; Num 9:8; 15:34.   92,207-08.

Luke 10:7
Confusion of personal and demonstrative pronoun; cf. Ps.-J. Num
24:19.   92,97-98.

Luke 10:9
See Tgs. for sense of *ēggiken*; e.g. Tg. Gen 11:4; 20:6; Ps.-J.
Gen 37:41.   92,208-11.

Luke 10:16
Play on Aramaic *qbl*; cf. Tgs. Deut 18:18-19.   86,371; 99,376-78.

Luke 10:18-19
Cf. targumic understanding of Gen 3:15.   254.

Luke 10:21
Targumic manner of expression.   272,95-96.

Luke 10:23-24
See Pal. Tg. Gen 49:18; also Tg. Isa 52:13-15; 35:5; Ps.-J. Num
24:3, 4, 15; Gen 49:1; Frg. Num 24:3, 15.   138,173; 267,243-45;
112,307; 198; 267,240-45; 272,139-40.

Luke 11:2-4
Expressions common to Tgs. and the Lord's Prayer; e.g. Neof. Exod
32:31; Gen 18:20-26; Ps.-J. Exod 17:11 etc.   92,298; 141,209;
272,115-19.

Luke 11:3
On *epiousios*, cf. Tgs. for similar expressions.   92,203-07; 200,
74-75.

Luke 11:27
Cf. Pal. Tg. Gen 49:25.   267,131-33; 248,246; 286,286; 230,51;
234,47.

Luke 11:41
Zk' = "to do good," "to give alms"; Pael: "to cleanse"; cf. Tg.
Ps 78:13.   178,321.

Luke 11:51
Tg. portrayal of Cain and Abel.   Tg. Lam 2:20 and the identification
of Zechariah.   224,31-36; 248,248; 138,164; 200,86-88; 4.

Luke 12:6, 8-9
Reverential manner of speaking of God reflects targumic practice.
272,93-95.

Luke 12:37-38
Messiah comes at night; cf. Pal. Tg. Exod 12:42.   256,202.

Luke 12:46
Dichotomēsei; cf. Tg. Isa 53:12.   92,256-57.

Luke 12:51
Eirēnēn dounai a semitic idiom; cf. Tg. Josh 9:15.   92,133.

Luke 13:4
Debt for sin; cf. Neof. Exod 32:31; Gen 18:20-26.   272,120.

Luke 13:9
Karpon poiein a Hebrew and Aramaic idiom; cf. Tg. Gen 1:11, 12;
Jer 17:8.   92,138-39.

Luke 13:24
'škḥ = "to find" and "to be able"; cf. 1QapGen 21:13.   236,389; 92,
133-34.

Luke 13:29
Notou may refer to the sea and to the south; cf. MT and Tg. Isa
49:12; Ps 107:3.   200,76-77.

Luke 13:33
Sēmeron kai aurion; Cf. Ps.-J. Gen 39:10.   92,299.

Luke 13:35
Messianic character of Tg. Ps 118:23-29.   213,249 (ET:259).

Luke 14:12
Poiein; cf. Frg. Gen 29:22.   92,302.

Luke 14:34, 35
Ry'' = "dung" (*korpian*) in Ps.-J., Pal. Tg., Tg. Ket.   92,167.

Luke 15:10
Reverential manner of speaking of God reflects targumic practice.
272,93-94.

Luke 15:11-32
See Ps.-J. Lev 6:5-6; Gen 27:15; 37:28; 27:27. 127,111-24.

Luke 15:18, 21
Reverential manner of speaking of God reflects targumic practice.
272,93-94.

Luke 16:9, 11, 13
For *mamōnas*, see CTg.C Gen 34:23. 92,139-40; 172,90.

Luke 16:15
See Onq. Gen 44:16. 178,328.

Luke 16:16
See Tg. Exod 19:21, 24 and LXX. 119,292.288.

Luke 16:19-31
Lack of hospitality; cf. Ps.-J. Gen 18:20. Naming of rich men
in some versions, a targumism. 127,88; 234,24.

Luke 17:20-21
Popular expectation as expressed in Ps.-J. Exod 12:42 and Tg.
Ps 116:13 rejected; cf. also Onq., Neof. Exod 17:7. 326; 327;
329; 230,284-85.

Luke 17:26-30
Targumic traditions associate judgment with Noah and Lot. 315.

Luke 18:4
Eipen en heauto; cf. Frg. Gen 44:18. 92,302.

Luke 18:18-30
The Shema in the Tgs. 272,125.

Luke 18:20
The Decalogue in the Tgs. 150.

Luke 18:32-33
See Tg. Hos 6:1-2. 95,5-7.

Luke 9:11
Revelation of the Messiah and of the kingdom in the Tgs.; e.g. Tg.
Isa 24:23. 272,140; 267,251.

Luke 19:17-19
Krkyn = "talents" or "cities"; *kar^e kha* = "Rome" in Ps.-J. Num 24:19.
92,2-3.

Luke 19:18
Poiein karpous; cf. Onq. Gen 49:15, 21. 92,302; 236,391.

Luke 19:38
Tg. Gen 49:10-12 and messianism. 82,21; 195,22-32.

Luke 20:9-19
Word play on *'bn, bn* in Tg. Ps 118:22.   358; 95,11-14.

Luke 20:20-26
Resurrection of the dead; cf. Neof. Gen 19:26 etc.   138,176-77.

Luke 20:42
Mry' as a title for God in 11QtgJob 24:7.   248,249.

Luke 20:46
Stolē also in Onq.   21,465.

Luke 21:8
See Tgs. for sense of *ēggiken*; e. g. Tg. Gen 11:4; 20:6; Ps.-J.
Gen 37:41.   92,208-11.

Luke 21:25-36
Eschatological theme; cf. Pal. Tg. Exod 12:42.   230,253; 121,40-41.

Luke 21:25-27
Theophany of Sinai in Tgs.   303,242-43.

Luke 21:29-31
Play on *qyṣ* with reference to the Messiah; cf. Pal. Tg. Gen 49:1;
Tg. Jer 8:20.   297; 245,45-46.

Luke 22:7
Day of unleavened bread; cf. Ps.-J. Lev 23:11; Num 28:18.   213,11
(ET:17).

Luke 22:14-16
Passover night and the coming of the Messiah; Frg. Exod 12:42.
189,77-78.

Luke 22:15
Phagein to pascha = "to eat this lamb"; cf. Tg. Exod 12:11, 43-46;
Num 9:10-11; Deut 16:2-3, 7 etc.   85; 213,155 (ET:162).

Luke 22:16
For notion of fulfillment, cf. Tg. Ezek 27:3; 28:12; Gen 2:1.   Use
of divine passive in Tgs.   92,232-33; 213,194-95 (ET:202).

Luke 22:19
Akedah, Passover and Tamid; Tg. Exod 12:42.   138,162-63; 241,27; 10.

Luke 22:20
Pal. Tg. Gen 40:23; Deut 32:1.   248,246; 138,166; 213,236 (ET:245).

Luke 22:27
See Ps.-J. Exod 18:12.   248,271.

Luke 22:28-30
"Kingdom" and "house"; cf. Tg. 2 Sam 7:12-14; 1 Chr 17:7-14.   80,
238-39; 230,252.

Luke 22:31
Neof. Deut 33:8.   248,247.

Luke 22:42
Pal. Tg. Gen 40:23; Deut 32:1; "to taste the cup of death."   248,
246; 138,166; 226; 324; 92,298; 234,47.

Luke 22:63-64
Messiah to prophesy by smell; cf. Tg. Isa 11:3.   127,408.

Luke 23:2-7
Pal. Tg. Gen 49:10-12 and messianism.   138,167-69; 195,22-32; 144,
67-69.

Luke 23:2
Christon basilea and Tg. Exod 12:42.   230,229.

Luke 23:44
Night precedes salvation events. 230,257.

Luke 24:32
"To open the Scriptures"; cf. Neof. Gen 40:18.   249a,I 366.

Luke 24:51
Ascension and cloud symbolism.   256,220-25.

John 1:1-18
Commentary on Gen 1:1-5 after pattern of Pal. Tg. Gen 3:24.   The
illuminating Word of God; cf. Tg. Exod 12:42.   Memra of Yahweh
in Tgs. as creating and revealing.   Memra, Shekinah, Yekara.   102;
294,38; 241,29; 230,255; 286; 137,381-94; 18; 167,244-48; 86,370;
107,523-24; 271; 92,298-99; 257,251-63; 135,232; 138,170-71; 272,
101-06.

John 1:1-3
See Neof. Gen 1:1; Exod 12:42.   286,147; 272,103-04.

John 1:1
Memra and Logos.   247,10; 248,266-69; 138,170-72; 21,458-59; 141,
205-06; 257,254-55; 310; 86,370; 18; 271; 272,101-06.

John 1:5, 9
See first night in Pal. Tg. Exod 12:42.   138,172; 286,325; 137,
389; 230,256.

John 1:9-10
Pejorative sense of ^{c}ālam frequent in Pal. Tg.   138,172; 137,
389-90.

John 1:14
Tgs. and the notion of glory, esp. Tg. Isa 6:1-4; grace and truth.
Memra and Logos.   248,273; 138,171-72; 257,256-57; 233; 137,388-89;
272,104; 86,370; 107,33.

John 1:14, 17
Ḥǎsad ū-qěšūṭ in Pal. Tg.   New Law and Tg. Deut 30:12-13.   138,
172; 227,33; 272,98-101.

John 1:14, 18
On title "Son of God," see Neof. Gen 1:1.   138,173-74.

John 1:16
Word play in Aramaic; ḥsd', "grace" or "disgrace"; cf. Frg. Lev
20:17. 1; 92,75.

John 1:17
Tgs. on Law, ḥsd, 'mt,   294; 138,171-72; 137,388-89.

John 1:18
Tgs. reflected in representation of the vision of God, esp. Tg.
Isa 6:1-4. Also Tg. Gen 4:1; 3:6.   248,273; 257,256-59; 256,63.

John 1:19--2:12
Week of preparation for the gift of Torah on the third day in
Ps.-J. Exod 19 and 24.   248,269; 292,102; 319.

John 1:19-23
New exodus evoked at the beginning of public ministry.   230,310-11.

John 1:23
See Tg. Isa 40:3; 57:14.   177,1-7.

John 1:29, 36
See Ps.-J. Exod 1:15; Pal. Tg. Exod 34:7.   Isaac typology and the
Lamb of God; cf. Neof. Gen 22:8; Tg. Lev 9:3; 22:27.   Messianic
association of ṭly', ^{c}bd, and 'bn by way of Tg. Ps 118:22-29;
Zech 3:8-9 is pre-Christian. 248,270-72; 230,131-212; 234,71;
228,563-74; 249a,I 212; 138,159; 257,255-56; 267,164-67; 342,93-94;
219; 108; 99a,92a.91b; 340,223-25; 7,217-27; 17.

John 1:31
Revelation of the Messiah in the Tgs.   272,140; 267,249.

John 1:32-33
Dove and the congregation of Israel; cf. Tg. Ps 68:14.   119,31.

John 1:48
See Tg. Cant 2:13.   257,257-58.

John 1:51
Possible reflection of Tg. Gen 28:10-17. Ladder of Jacob and
Sinai; Tg. Ps 68; Hag 1; Ps.-J. Deut 33:2, 15; Gen 49:25. 97,
123-27; 248,273; 257,258; 127,408; 111,375; 272,146-47; 292,75;
286,134-35.

John 2:1-11
Miryam and Mary; Tg. Num 20:29 etc. Sinai covenant and marriage;
Tg. Exod 19:5: *sgwlh--ḥbybyn*. Abundance of new wine; cf. Tg. Lev
26:10. Jewish traditions.   257,261-62; 231; 292,110; 286,411; 321.

John 2:5
See Tg. Exod 19:8; 24:7, etc. 292,46-47.

John 2:10
Messianic wine preserved for the just; cf. Ps.-J. Gen 27:25; Tg.
Cant 8:2. 249a,I 261.

John 2:11
Tgs. and the notion of glory, esp. Tg. Isa 6:1-4. See use of
'tgly in Tg. Exod 19:9, 11. 248,269.273; 257,256-57; 292,25.70.

John 2:16-17
Tg. Isa 56:1-9; 57:19 reflect Exod 21:1--22:23--*seder* and *haptara*.
Influence of synagogue readings. 299.

John 2:22
"To remember"; cf. Neof., Frg. Gen 40:23. 248,257.

John 3:5
Paschal background to new birth in baptism. 230,256.

John 3:10
"Teacher of Israel"; e.g. Ps.-J. Deut 32:3; 34:5. 99a,119a.

John 3:11-13
See Tg. Gen 4:1; 3:6; Deut 30:11-14. 257,258-59; 227,33; 256,63;
234,44; 99a,123a.

John 3:14-15
Zqp in double sense: Tg. 1 Chr 10:12; Esth I 9:13; II 7:10; or
ystlq. Spiritualization; cf. Neof., Ps.-J., Frg. Num 21:4-9;
Ps.-J. Exod 15:25; Tg. Gen 3:15. Cf. also Tg. Isa 53:13; Hos 6:1-2.
92,141; 93; 141,201; 267,145-49; 35; 99,378; 234,55-56; 272,163;
257,262-63; 258,509; 127,148; 99a,319ab; 279,157; 86,370; 107,133;
272,147-48.

John 3:16
Isaac typology; cf. Tg. Lev 22:27.   257,255-56; 118,68; 230,204;
234,55; 340.

John 3:19
True light; paschal background.   230,256.

John 3:31
"From the earth," "from above"; cf. Ps.-J. Gen 27:28; Frg. Gen
40:23.   92,147-48; 249a,I 367.

John 4
See Neof. Exod 15:27.   230,325.

John 4:7-15
Symbolism of well in Tg. Gen 28:2-3; 10-22; 29; Num 21:16-18.
248,274-75; 257,261; 292,162-69; 132,76-77; 294,219-20; 330; 331;
111; 131,339; 210; 100; 272,145-56.

John 4:10-12
"To draw water" = "to acquire knowledge of the Law"; Tg. Isa 12:3;
8:6; Cant 4:15.   292,129; 248,275-76.

John 4:12
Patriarchs called "father"; Jacob's signs; cf. Ps.-J. Frg. Gen
28:10.   292,140.169-70; 30,10.12.22; 32,22; 234,55; 210,70; 107,
170-71.

John 4:23-24
"Worship in spirit and in truth" a Christian amplification of
plḥ bqwšṭ.   287; 272,125-27.

John 4:24
God as Spirit in Pal. Tg.   272,112-13.

John 4:25
Confusion of *ntn* and *tny*; examples of *tny* from Neof.   236,392.

John 4:35
White for maturity; cf. Onq. Gen 29:12.   21,479-80.

John 5:28
Resurrection in the Pal. Tg.   138,176-77.

John 5:37-38
Manifestation of Sinai a manifestation of the Word; Ps.-J., Neof.
Deut 4:12-14.   286,479-80.

John 6--7
Manna and rock connected in Exod 16-17 and Tgs.   99a,195a.

John 6

Midrashic traditions about the manna in the Tgs.; cf. Tg. Num
1:6-7; Ps.-J. Exod 16; Pal. Tg. Num 22:28; Tg. Josh 5 etc.   248,
277-78; 141,208-09; 276; 257,262; 239; 276,42-93; 230,206-07.

John 6:15

Pal. Tg. Gen 49:10-12 and messianism.   138,167-69; 99a,182b-183a;
195,22-32; 144,67-69.

John 6:31-35, 41, 48, 50-51

Moses as the bread in Onq., Neof., Ps.-J. Exod 16:15.   Manna
traditions in Judaism; Neof. Num 21:4-9; Tg. Josh 5:12; Ps 78:24.
349; 248,278; 276,102-06; 99a,62b.197ab.200ab; 294,227-28; 177,
11-16; 258,502.

John 6:41-43, 58-61

Ps.-J. Num 11:6-7 and ingratitude of Israel.   242.

John 6:45

See Tg. Isa 54:13; Jer 31:34.   177,17-20; 294,229.

John 6:49

See Tg. Num 21:5-6.   234,56.

John 6:51-56

"Flesh" for "body."   10; 213,191-94 (ET:198-201).

John 7:2, 14

Feast of Tabernacles; cf. Tg. Lev 23:43; Ps.-J. Exod 12:37; 13:20.
257,253.

John 7:18

Son considers glory of his father in Pal. Tg. Gen 32:7(8), 11(12);
Lev 19:3.   272,142.

John 7:23

See Ps.-J. Gen 22:1.   248,254.

John 7:27

Origin of Messiah and Pal. Tg. Exod 12:42.   138,169-70; 257,258-59;
195,31-32.

John 7:33-35

Slq in Tgs. means both "to ascend" and "to depart."   35.

John 7:37-38

Various targumic references suggested; e.g. Tg. Cant 4:15; Neof.
Num 21:19; Ps.-J. Num 21:16, 4-9; Tg. Pss 78:16; 46:5-8; Ps.-J. Num
20:2; Tg. Ezek 47:1-12; Zech 14:8.   248,275-77; 177,21-38; 257,260-61;
99a,62b; 294,255-56; 330; 331; 86,371; 98; 191; 99,375-76; 192; 196;
107,322; 129,165-66; 272,146.

John 7:40-44
Messianic sense of Tg. Mic 5:1, 3.   123.

John 7:42
Hò Christos in John close to several Tg. passages in prophets;
see also Ps.-J. Gen 35:21; Tg. Mic 5:1.   177,39-59; 284,52-53; 34,
99-101.

John 7:53--8:11
See Onq. Exod 23:1-7.   127,180-83.

John 8
Abraham and Isaac in Tgs.   Paschal theology and Tg. Exod 12:42.
138,159.167; 228,563-74.

John 8:12
See Ps.-J. Exod 13:21; Neof. Exod 33:14; Neof., Onq. Deut 1:33;
paschal background; illuminating Word of God; Tg. Exod 12:42.   257,
257; 230,256; 241,29.

John 8:28
Zqp in double sense, Tg. 1 Chr 10:10; Esth I 9:13; II 7:10; or
ystlq.   92,141; 267,145-49; 141,201; 35; 272,163.

John 8:31-59
The paternity of Abraham and of the devil and the feast of Tabernacles in Jewish tradition; see esp. Tg. Gen 15; 3; 4; Ps 118.
279; 335,119-22.

John 8:32
See Tg. Lev 23:43; Ps.-J. Exod 12:37; 13:20; Neof. Gen 15:11 etc.
257,253.258-59; 311; 335,76-82.92.

John 8:35
Tg. evidence for "house" as "family."   335,179-82; 80,237-38.

John 8:36
Isaac typology; see Tg. Lev 22:27.   257,255-56.

John 8:38-45
See Pal. Tg. Gen 5:3; 3:6; 4:1-2.   131,342; 132,79-80; 104,132-41;
248,280-81; 234,59-61; 106,45.179; 107,358; 115,79; 224,31-36;
351; 190; 207.

John 8:41
"Born of prostitution"; see Ps.-J. Gen 5:3; 4:1 concerning the
birth of Cain.   99a,239a.

John 8:44
Ps.-J. Gen 4:1-8 an early tradition; also Ps.-J. Gen 3:6.   182;
115; 230,255; 272,121.

John 8:51-53
Possible influence of Neof. Gen 3:22. 99a,245a.

John 8:56
See Neof. Gen 49:18. Isaac typology; see Tg. Lev 22:27. Seeing
the days of the Messiah; Tg. Gen 4:1; 3:6; 15:12, 17. See Gen
17:17; 18:12 and Tgs. Cf. also Tg. Isa 52:13-15; 35:5; 43:8-13;
Pal. Tg. Num 24:3, 4, 15. 138,173; 257,255-59; 258,503; 267,
240-45; 272,144-45; 107,360; 99a,245b; 248,279; 198; 199,109.

John 8:58
See Tg. Isa 43:10-11. 230,229.

John 8:59
Stoning; see Cain and Abel in Ps.-J. Gen 4:8. 115,78.

John 9
Illumination as paschal theme. 230,256.

John 9:7
See Tg. Cant 4:15. 257,260-61; 248,275-76.

John 10:31
Stoning; see Cain and Abel in Ps.-J. Gen 4:8. 115,78.

John 10:34
Tg. Ps 82:6 avoids human equality with God. 177,60-65; but cf.
162,329-32.

John 11:8
Stoning; Cain and Abel in Ps.-J. Gen 4:8. 115,78.

John 11:43
"To call with a loud voice"; cf. Sam. Tg. Num 24:10. 86,371.

John 11:51
Holy spirit, prophecy and sanctuary in Tgs. 14,206-07; 249,281-83.

John 12:13
Tg. Gen 49:10-12 and messianism. Messianic character of Tg. Ps
118:23-29. 82,21; 195,22-32; 213,249 (ET:259).

John 12:16
See Neof., Frg. Gen 40:23. 248,257.

John 12:27
See prayer of Tamar in Ps.-J. Gen 38:25. 272,143-44.

John 12:27-30
Bath qol and Tgs.; e.g. Pal. Tg. Gen 38:26. 272,113-14.

John 12:32, 34
Zqp or *ystlq* in double sense, Tg. 1 Chr 10:12; Esth I 9:13; II
7:10.   92,141; 267,145-49; 93,7; 273; 141,201; 35; 272,163.

John 12:38-40
Cf. Tg. Isa 6:1-10; John responsible for form of quotation.   177,
99-103; 258,504.

John 12:40-41
See Tg. Isa 52:13-15; 35:5; Pal. Tg. Num 24:3, 4, 15.   198.

John 12:41
Tgs. and glory as substitute for the divine name, esp. Tg. Isa
6:1-4.   248,273; 92,79; 141,202; 178,212; 257,256-57; 272,98-100;
267,41; 107,486-87; 317,520.

John 12:48-50
See Tg. Isa 6:1-5; Neof., Ps.-J. Deut 18:18-19.   257,256-57; 99a,
63a.315b; 86,371-72; 99,376-78; 107,492.

John 13--17
On farewell discourse genre, see Pal. Tg. Gen 49:1-2; Deut 33.
141,204; 112.

John 13:1-17
Purification before farewell discourses.   112,309-23.452.

John 13:8
On reward in the world to come, see Tg. Gen 15:1.   99a,336b.

John 13:10
Application of concept *pswl* from Tgs. to Judas.   112,474-81.

John 13:30
Paschal background for the theme of "night."   230,256.

John 14--17
Promises of Tg. Exod 29:42-46 fulfilled.   286,380-82.

John 14:1-3
Leadership of Moses and heavenly temple; cf. Neof. Exod 15:13, 17;
Ps.-J. Deut 33:21; 1:29, 32-33; Frg. Exod 12:42.   "Kingdom" and
"house"; cf. Tg. 2 Sam 7:12-14; 1 Chr 17:9-10.   99a,349ab; 80,238.

John 14:2-3
See Ps.-J. Exod 13:21; Neof. Exod 33:14; Neof., Onq. Deut 1:33.
257,257; 272,142-43.

John 14:8-11
God, Memra and mutual indwelling; Tg. Num 14:21.   286,443-44.

John 14:11
See Neof. Deut 32:29.   286,407.

John 14:26
Cf. *rūḥq dĕ-qudša* in the Tgs.   138,173; 137,394-96.

John 14:31
Isaac typology; see Tg. Lev 22:27.   257,255-56.

John 15
See symbolism of vine in Tg. Ps 80:11-12.   294,429.

John 15:2, 4, 5, 8, 16
Karpon pherein (?) a Hebrew and Aramaic idiom; cf. Tg. Gen 1:11,
12; Jer 17:8.   92,138-39; 236,391.

John 15:26
Cf. *rūḥa dĕ-qudša* in the Tgs.   138,173; 137,394-96.

John 16:4b-16
Paraclete; cf. Tg. Job 33:23.   99a,385a.

John 16:13-15
Cf. *rūḥa dĕ-qudša* in the Tgs.   138,173; 137,394-96.

John 16:13
Anaggellein: ḥwy or *tny* = "to explain, teach."   236,292.

John 16:32
Zech 13:7 in Tg. Isa 53:6.   19,81-82.123.

John 17
Tg. Exod 19--20 and covenant context.   281.

John 17:8
See Tg. Deut 18:18-19.   86,371; 99,377.

John 17:24
Vision of God and notion of glory; cf. Tg. Isa 6:1-5; Neof. Gen
45:13.   257,256-57; 272,142.

John 18:10
Proper name a targumism.   234,24; 246,516.

John 18:11
"To taste the cup of death"; cf. Pal. Tg. Gen 40:23; Deut 32:1.
248,246; 138,166; 226; 325; 3,195; 92,233.

John 18:12, 24
Cf. the binding of Isaac.   212,380-85.

John 18:28
Paschal lamb in Pal. Tg.   230,202.

John 18:29-37
Pal. Tg. Gen 49:10-12 and messianism. 138,167-69; 195,22-32; 144,
67-69.

John 18:31
Ṣlb in Tgs. and crucifixion. 151.

John 19:6
Ṣlb in Tgs. and crucifixion. 151.

John 19:24
See Tg. Ps 22:19. 177,99-103.

John 19:25-27
Miryam and Mary; Tg. Num 20:29 etc. 275,261-62; 231; 321; 234,58.

John 19:31
Burial by sunset; cf. Ps.-J. Deut 21:23; Neof. Num 25:4. 99a,448b;
359,94.

John 19:34
Blood and water in Ps.-J. Num 20:11. 248,277; 257,260; 294,
255-56; 330; 331; 230,39.332; 98,539-40.

John 19:36
Paschal lamb in Jewish liturgy. 230,202.

John 19:37
Spiritualization; cf. Ps.-J., Frg. Num 21:4-8. 257,262-63.

John 20:16
Strapheisa possibly represents Aramaic "to recognize"; cf. Ps.-J.
Gen 4:15. *Rabbouni, rabbounei* in Pal. Tg. 92,23-24.44-46.255-56;
236,395; 86,363; 135,231; 234,47; 21; 107,991; 216.

John 20:23
Targumic use of *šry, šbq, nṭr*; e.g. Neof. Gen 4:7; *ptḥ* and *'ḥd*
in Tg. Isa 22:22. 235,177-78; 248,246; 138,163-64; 351,95.102.
121-24; 99a,472b; 86,368; 163; 107,1039-40; 332,192-93; 272,129-30;
135,231; 350,65.

Acts
Reflection of Tgs. in speeches of Acts; little emphasis on expiation.
278.

Acts 1:4
Synalizomenos: Tg. Ps 141:4. 356,106-09.

Acts 1:6
Pal. Tg. Gen 49:10-12 and messianism. Tg. 2 Sam 7:11; 1 Sam 1:35 and
the notion of the kingdom. 138,167-69; 80,218; 195,22-32; 144,67-69.

Acts 1:9
Ascension and cloud symbolism. 256,220-25; 345,187.

Acts 1:14
Homothymadon and notion of *ekklēsia*; cf. Tg. Exod 19:1, 3. 227,37;
141,208.

Acts 1:15-26
Pal. Tg. Gen 44:18 source of quotation in v 17. 357.

Acts 1:21-22
"Witnesses"; cf. Tg. Num 10:31. 234,48.

Acts 2--3
Feast of Weeks in Tgs. as feast of Covenant and Law. 248,260;
138,165-66; 141,207-08; 303; 227; 290.

Acts 2:1
Epi to auto and the notion of *ekklēsia*; cf. Tg. Exod 19:1, 3.
227,37.

Acts 2:3
Holy spirit as source of tongues and fire; cf. Frg. Num 11:26;
11QtgJob 41:11. Tg. Isa 28:10-13 and tongues. 356,101-02; 248,
260; 89.

Acts 2:9-11
Languages listed and those of OT Tgs. 40,147-48.

Acts 2:24
See Tg. Ps 18:5; 2 Sam 22:5. 255,43-44.

Acts 2:40
Cf. Tg. Ps 11:8. 356,30.

Acts 2:42
Breaking of bread; cf. Tg. 1 Sam 9:13. 213,114 (ET:120).

Acts 2:46
Israel in Tgs. as holy *kenista*; cf. notion of *ekklēsia*. 141,208.

Acts 3:13
Paterōn (pl.) reflects Sam. Pent. and Sam. Tg. Exod 3:6. 356,29-30;
355,22-24.

Acts 3:14
Atoning of just man; Pal. Tg. Gen 22:14. 351,126.

Acts 3:22, 23
See Tgs. Deut 18:19. 128.

Acts 3:25-26
Redemption by Christ and the sacrifice of Isaac. 340,221.

Acts 4:11
Tg. Ps 118:22--leaders reject *ṭly* . 200,173; 212,374-76; 95,11-14;
160,310.

Acts 4:13
Idiōtēs: cf. Frg. Gen 28:17. 356,101.

Acts 4:27
Spirit of God in the Tgs. 251,146-52.

Acts 4:32
Notion of *ekklēsia*; cf. Tg. Exod 19:1, 3. 227,36-37; 141,208.

Acts 5:12
Israel in Tgs. as a holy *kenista*; cf. notion of *ekklēsia*. 141,208.

Acts 5:30
Hanging on a tree = crucifixion in Neof. Gen 40:19; 41:13; Tg. Deut
21:22-23. 138,183; 359,88-94.

Acts 7
Reflects targumic traditions, esp. about Moses. 235,165; 7,212-23;
279,115; 6; 245,49.

Acts 7:2
Targumic expression of revelation. See also 1QapGen 22:27. 272,
99; 236,390; 90,666; 91; 86,372.

Acts 7:3
See Ps.-J. Gen 12:1. 356,26-27.159; 355,16-17.

Acts 7:4
See Sam. Pent. and Sam. Tg. Gen 11:32 for Abraham's age. 356,
28-29.159; 355,21-22.

Acts 7:5
See Sam. Pent. and Sam. Tg. Deut 2:5 rather than MT or LXX: one
Sam. text is Aramaic. 356,27.195; 355,17-19.

Acts 7:10
Hēgoumenon: cf. Ps.-J., Neof. Gen 41:41-43. 238,19; 356,27-28.159;
355,19-21.

Acts 7:20-41
Moses and Jonah as figures of Christ. 234,45.

Acts 7:32
Paterōn (pl.) reflects Sam. Pent. and Sam. Tg. Exod 3:6. 356,29-30;
355,22-24.

Acts 7:48
Shekinah and "the work of your hands"; cf. Ps.-J., Neof. m. Exod
39:43. 232,86-87.

Acts 7:52
Atoning of just man; Pal. Tg. Gen 22:14. 351,126.

Acts 8:2
Poiein kopeton frequent in Tgs.; cf. Tg. Jer 48:38; Ezek 27:37;
Amos 5:16; Mic 1:11. 356,136-37.

Acts 8:22
Metanoein apo: cf. Frg. Gen 18:21; 19:24; Exod 10:28; 14:29; Tg.
Jer 8:6; 18:8; Job 36:10; Ezek 33:12. 356,102-05.

Acts 8:32
See Tg. Isa 53:7-8. 356,31.

Acts 8:39
Poreuthēnai tina tēn hodon autou: cf. Frg. Gen 4:7; Onq. Gen 32:1.
356,137-38.

Acts 8:40
Heurethēnai eis: cf. Frg. Gen 28:10. 356,100.

Acts 10:34-35
Tg. Isa 56:1-9; 57:19 reflect Exod 21:1--22:23--*seder* and *haptara*.
Influence of synagogue readings. 299.

Acts 10:38
Spirit of God in Tgs. 251,146-52.

Acts 10:39
Hanging on a tree = crucifixion in Neof. Gen 40:19; 41:13; cf.
debate over Deut 21:22-23 in Judaism. 138,183; 359,88-94.

Acts 11:15-18
Possession of the Spirit a sign of God's people; cf. Ps.-J. Exod
33:16. 272,109.

Acts 13:11
Citation reflects Tg. Ps 58:9. 356,24-25.89; 355,11-13.

Acts 13:18
Etropophorēsen: see use of *swpyq ̣qwrk'* in Tgs. 186,285-87.

Acts 13:22
Tg. 1 Sam 13:14 preferable to MT or LXX Isa 44:28. 356,21-24.52.54.
120.161-62; 160,307; 355,5-11.

Acts 13:28-30
See Tgs. Deut 21:22-23. 359,91-93.

Acts 13:32-37
Messianic interpretation in Tg. Ps 80:6; cf. targumic treatment of
Ps 2:7.   255,21.

Acts 13:34
See Tg. Isa 55:3; Jer 33:15; Onq. Gen 49:10.   255,48-81.

Acts 14:10
Anastēnai epi tous podas: cf. Pal. Tg. Gen 38:26.   356,133-34.

Acts 15:14
"A people for his name" a targumic expression; cf. Tg. Zech 2:15.
117; 86,372; 156,364-65.

Acts 17:3
"To open the Scriptures"; cf. Neof. Gen 40:18.   249a,I 366.

Acts 19:44-48
Possession of the Spirit a sign of God's people; cf. Ps.-J. Exod
33:16.   272,109.

Acts 22:14
Atoning of just man; Pal. Tg. Gen 22:14.   351,126.

Acts 23:6, 10
Resurrection of the dead; cf. Neof. Gen 19:26 etc.   138,176-77.

Acts 24:15
Resurrection of the dead; cf. Neof. Gen 19:26.   138,176-77.

Acts 26:16
Anastēnai epi tous podas: cf. Pal. Tg. Gen 38:26.   356,133-34.

Acts 26:18
See Tg. Isa 9:1; Ps 18:29.   230,232-36.

Acts 26:24
Paul's madness and Balaam (Ps.-J. Num 22:5).   341,128-29.

Rom 1:2
Tgs. and spirit of holiness.   141,206.

Rom 1:17
Tg. and Qumran on Hab 2:4.   347,48-49.

Rom 2:1
See Tg. Gen 38:26; Lev 26:43; Frg., Neof. Num 12:15; Ps.-J. Num
12:14.   248,246; 256,141.

Rom 2:4-6
Delay of punishment for repentance; see Neof. Gen 4:7; 18:21; Tg.
Hab 3:1.   303,171; 234,67.

Rom 3:5

See Tg. Ps 51:6.   263,197.

Rom 3:23

Paradise as place of Shekinah; Neof. Gen 3:24; Ps.-J. Gen 2:25.
Garments of glory.   263,220; 272,120-21; 230,230.

Rom 3:24

Justification by grace or works; cf. Pal. Tg. Gen 4:8.   86,372-73;
130,134-36.

Rom 3:25

Proetheto; cf. Tg. Gen 22:8.   230,205; 228,571-72; 116,24.

Rom 3:26

Delay of punishment for repentance, see Neof. Gen 4:7; 18:21; Tg.
Hab 3:1.   303,171.

Rom 4:3

On merits of Abraham, see Onq., Ps.-J. Gen 15:6; Tg. Ps 106:31.
103,110; 263,261.

Rom 4:15

See Tg. Gen 2:15; 3:23.   263,281.

Rom 4:17

See Frg. Exod 12:42; Ps.-J. Gen 22:5.   263,290; 230,205.

Rom 4:20

Abraham's laugh as exultation in Tg. Gen 17:17.   263,293.

Rom 4:25

On use of Tg. Isa 53:5, 12; Hos 6:1-2; Gen 22:5.   295,273-78; 93;
230,205.

Rom 5:12-21

God's justice and love in Tg. Gen 4:3-16.   Jewish background; e.g.
Ps.-J. Gen 3:6.   Tg. on Ten Words.   New Adam in Pal. Tg.   351,
124-26; 277; 303,297; 130,133-34; 121,54; 138,181; 230,254.

Rom 5:12

Death because of homicide and adultery in Tg. Exod 20:13.   86,373;
130,133-34.

Rom 6

NT paschal theology and Tg. Exod 12:42.   138,167; 230,256.

Rom 6:3-4

Circumcision and baptism; Tg. Exod 4:24-26; Gen 17:26; Exod 12:13;
Ezek 16:6.   New life; paschal background.   338; 339; 138,162;
242,36-38; 86,374-75; 230,254.256.

Rom 7
Adam and Moses; Jewish background.   230,254; 234,61; 261.

Rom 7:7
Adam and the Law in Paradise; see Tg. Gen 3:23; 2:15.   Sin as
concupiscence; see Neof. Exod 20:17; Deut 5:18.   264,91.104-05;
260,521; 262,159-64; 303,290.

Rom 7:9
Goodness of the Law; see Tg. Gen 3:23; Neof. Gen 2:15.   264,116.

Rom 7:12
"Goodness" of the Law; cf. Tg. Gen 3:23.   261,139.

Rom 8:6
"Flesh" and "spirit"; cf. Tg. Gen 6:3.   131,78-79.

Rom 8:15
Tgs. reticent about calling God Father; cf. Tg. Mal 1:6; Jer 3:4.
264,279.

Rom 8:19-22
Messianic expectation.   230,254.

Rom 8:29
Image of God and creation.   230,256.

Rom 8:32
Akedah and Isaac typology; Frg., Neof. Exod 12:42; Neof. Gen 22:14.
118,67; 116; 264,279; 230,204; 234,55; 340,218.

Rom 8:33-34
See Tg. Isa 50:4-8; 53:13.   201,35-36; 19,94.

Rom 9:7-11
Abraham and Isaac in the Tgs.   138,159.167; 228,4.

Rom 10:3
Confidence in works in the Pal. Tgs.   234,62.

Rom 10:6-8
Pal. Tg. Deut 30:12-14; cf. Ps.-J. Exod 19:18; Tg. Ps 68:18.   267,
70-78; 248,253; 18; 246,514; 138,155-56; 238,31; 257,258-59; 227,
33; 212,379-80; 95,8-9; 256,63; 265,103-06; 303,197; 158,54-55;
286,500-01; 259; 230,319-20; 234,44.

Rom 10:7
Citation as in Frg. Deut 30:13.   201,146.

Rom 10:11
Messianic interpretation in Tg. Isa 28:16.   158,57.

Rom 10:14-21
Cf. refusal of Law in Tg. Deut 33:2.   303,258-59.

Rom 10:16
Justification by grace or works; cf. Pal. Tg. Gen 4:8.   86,372-73;
130,134-36.

Rom 11:9
Sacrificial table; cf. Tg. Ps 68:23.   265,119.

Rom 11:16
Cf. Onq. Deut 32:14 with Ps.-J., Frg. Deut 32:14; see also Frg.
Num 15:20; Tg. Isa 11:1, 10; 53:2.   201,106-12.

Rom 11:26
Messianic interpretation in Tg. Isa 11.   158,57.

Rom 11:28
Merits of patriarchs; Neof. Gen 12:3; 18:18; 26:24 etc.   138,
181-82.

Rom 11:35
Sense of verse same as Tg. Job 41:11.   201,129.

Rom 12:1
Presence of God in synagogue and the church as temple; Frg. Exod
20:21.   350,84.

Rom 12:12
Paul's expression for acceptable sacrifice found in Neof. Exod
29:18; Lev 1:9, 13, 17; 2:9; 3:5 etc.   248,255-56.

Rom 12:19
See Onq., Ps.-J., Frg. Deut 32:35.   265,106; 158,144.

Rom 13:14
"Put on Christ"; cf. garment of glory in Tg. Gen 3:21.   230,257.

Rom 15:12
Messianic interpretation in Tg. Isa 11.   158,57.

Rom 16:20
Collective sense of "seed" in Tg. Gen 3:15.   24.

1 Cor 2:7-10
See Tg. Isa 52:13-15; 35:5; Pal. Tg. Num 24:3, 4, 15.   198.

1 Cor 5:7
Passover and covenant; Akedah; Tg. Lev 26:42; 22:27; Neof. Gen
18:6.   241,37.

1 Cor 5:8
Abraham as totally "unleavened," i.e. pure, in CTg.F Lev 22:26-28.
230,173.

1 Cor 6:16
Citation of Gen 2:24 and Tgs. 119,81.

1 Cor 7:14
Neof. Gen 3:16 and the husband's power over the wife for justification and sin. 138,182.

1 Cor 7:31
"New world"; cf. eschatological ideas of Pal. Tg. 230,253.

1 Cor 9:8-10
See Ps.-J. Deut 25:4; literal meaning extended. 201,161-66.

1 Cor 10:3
Manna prefigures the Eucharist; Tg. Josh 5. 239; 276,94-99.

1 Cor 10:4
Tg. Num 21; Exod 17:9; Num 20:2-12. 235,177; 138,156; 141,209;
257,260-61; 234,54; 191,372; 292,163-69; 111,373; 210; 135,231-32;
349; 248,278; 265,106; 330; 331; 86,373-74; 158,66-70; 196; 259,
504-05.

1 Cor 10:6
Sin as concupiscence; cf. Tg. Gen 3:6. 260,501.

1 Cor 10:14-21
See Tg. Deut 32:14 in Onq., Ps.-J., and Frg. 201,115.

1 Cor 11:4, 6
Brys̆ gly expresses liberation in Tg. Gen 40:18; Exod 14:8; Lev
26:13; Num 33:3. 248,255; 138,183.

1 Cor 11:24-26
See Neof. Exod 12:42; notion of anamnēsis; also Ps.-J., Onq. Exod
12:14; 13:9. Blood and covenant; Tg. Lev 26:42; 22:27; Neof. Gen
18:6; Onq., Ps.-J. Exod 24:8. 241,27.37; 213,236 (ET:245).218;
230,71; 340,225-27.

1 Cor 14:20-21
Tg. Isa 28:7-13 and tongues. 89.

1 Cor 15:3
The use of Tg. Isa 53:5, 12. 295,273-78.

1 Cor 15:4
See Tg. Hos 6:1-2; Isa 53:12. Isaac typology probable. Jewish
traditions concerning the third day. 95,5-7; 93; 266; 118,71; 250,
262-90.

1 Cor 15:20-24
New Adam in the Pal. Tg.   230,254.

1 Cor 15:26
Paschal background for the destruction of death.   230,254.

1 Cor 15:45-49
See Neof. Gen 2:8.   286,170.

1 Cor 15:45
See reaction of Onq. and Pal. Tg. Gen 2:7; paschal background for
vivifying spirit.   121,44; 230,254.

1 Cor 15:52
Eschatological context of trumpet in Tg. Exod 19:13, 16, 19; 20:18.
303,104.265.

1 Cor 15:53-56
See Tg. Hos 13:14.   181,282-83.

2 Cor 1:6
Fixed time of redemption; cf. Neof. Gen 49:1.   249a,I 433.

2 Cor 3:7--4:6
Pal. Tg. Exod 33--34; Ps.-J. Num 7:89 and midrash on the veil of
Moses. *Bryš gly* expresses liberation in Tg. Gen 40:18; Exod 14:8;
Lev 26:13; Num 33:3.   267,168-88; 224,43-48; 234,41; 248,255; 246,
512.

2 Cor 3:7-18
Glory of Moses' face and veil in Pal. Tg.   234,61; 267,171-88;
205,386-94; 224,37-47.

2 Cor 3:12-18
See Ps.-J. Num 7:89; Exod 33:16; targumic background of *parrēsia*.
286,423; 337.

2 Cor 3:13
See Tg. Deut 34:7.   246,511.

2 Cor 3:14-16
See Ps.-J. Exod 33:5-8.   267,177-81.

2 Cor 3:16-18
See Tg. Exod 34:29.   286,387.

2 Cor 3:16
See Ps.-J. Exod 33:7 for *epistrepsē*.   138,165.

2 Cor 3:17
"The Lord is the Spirit" and Ps.-J. Num 7:80; Exod 33:11, 20.   267,
182-88; 272,110-13.

2 Cor 4:6
Illumination, baptism and paschal background.   230,256.

2 Cor 5:17
Paschal background for new creature.   230,254.256.

2 Cor 8:15
See Ps.-J. Exod 16:18.   201,174-77.

Gal 1:4
Reminiscence of Isaac in death of Christ.   230,204.

Gal 2:9
"Column"; cf. Tg. Num 20:29.   234,48.

Gal 2:20
Reminiscence of Isaac in the death of Christ.   230,204.

Gal 3:6-29
Redemption prefigured in Jewish development of Gen 12 etc.   340,
219-21.

Gal 3:10
See Pal. Tg. Deut 27:26; Onq. Lev 18:5.   201,46-47.

Gal 3:11
Tg. and Qumran on Hab 2:4.   347.

Gal 3:13
Hanging on a tree = crucifixion in Neof. Gen 40:19; 41:13.   See
Onq., Pal. Tg. Deut 21:22-23 and Jewish debate over meaning.
138,183; 201,48-51; 359.

Gal 3:16
Abraham and Isaac in the Tgs.   138,159.167; 158,70-73; 359,97-98;
228,566.

Gal 3:27
"To put on Christ"; influence of Tg. Gen 3:21.   230,257.

Gal 4:21--5:1
See Tg. Isa 54:1-3.   201,90-97.

Gal 4:21-31
Abraham and Isaac in the Tgs.   138,159.164-65; 224,37-41; 228,566;
234,61.

Gal 4:28-31
Cf. dispute of Isaac and Ishmael in Tg. Gen 22:1-10; also Tg.
Gen 21:10.   138,164-65; 234,61; 224,37-43; 248,254.

Gal 6:15
New creature; cf. creation and passover themes in Pal. Tg.   230,
254.256.

Eph 2:10
Re-creation; cf. creation and passover themes in Pal. Tg.   230,256.

Eph 2:11-22
Tg. Isa 56:1-9; 57:19 reflect Exod 21:1--22:23--*seder* and *haptara*;
influence of synagogue liturgy in the NT.   234,20; 299.

Eph 2:15
New man; cf. creation and passover themes in Pal. Tg.   230,254.256.

Eph 2:20-22
Presence of God in synagogue and the church as temple; Frg. Exod
20:21.   350,85.

Eph 3:10
See Ps.-J. Gen 22:11-12.   251,215.

Eph 4:8
Ps 68:19 cited according to Tg.   267,78-81; 235,55; 248,253; 362,
56; 138,156; 356,25-26.53; 238,28; 227,32-33; 212; 308; 303,196-97;
158,35-36.144; 202,5-7; 355,13-15; 259,504-05; 234,46.

Eph 4:22-25
See Pal. Tg. Gen 3:3-21; 48:22.   132,77-78; 131,340-41.

Eph 5:2
Jesus' obedience and Isaac's self-sacrifice.   230,204.

Eph 5:8-14
Illumination, paschal background.   See Tg. Isa 9:1; Ps 18:29.
230,256.232-36.

Eph 5:13
Citation of Gen 2:24 and Tgs.   119,81.

Eph 5:25
Jesus' obedience and Isaac's self-sacrifice.   230,204.

Phil 2:6-11
Humiliation-exaltation structure; cf. 1 Sam 2:7-10 and Tg.   278.

Phil 2:11
See Tg. Isa 45:23.   278.

Phil 3:2
"Dogs" for pagans in Neof. Exod 22:30.   138,184.

Phil 3:9
Targumic background for confidence in works.   234,62.

Phil 4:1
See Tg. Isa 28:5.   28,51-52.

Phil 4:18
Paul's expressions for acceptable sacrifice found in Neof. Exod
29:18; Lev 1:19, 13, 17; 2:9; 3:5 etc.   Spiritual sacrifices;
cf. Ps.-J. Exod 40:6; Tg. Hos 14:3.   248,255-56; 186,288.

Col 1:12
Illumination; paschal background.   230,256.

Col 1:13
See Tg. Isa 9:1; Ps 18:29.   230,232-36.

Col 1:15
See Tg. Exod 4:22; 11:1; Gen 1:1.   241,28.

Col 2:11-14
Circumcision and baptism; Tg. Exod 4:24-26.   338; 339; 138,162;
241,36-38; 86,374-75.

Col 2:14-15
See Ps.-J. Num 25:1-7; connected with Deut 21:23 in rabbinic
tradition.   201,4-7.

Col 3:10
Creation; paschal background in Pal. Tg.   230,252.256.275.

Col 3:13
On pardoning, cf. Tg. Deut 22:4.   234,68.

1 Thess 2:19
See Tg. Isa 28:5.   28,51-52.

1 Thess 4:15-17
Eschatological context for trumpet in Tg. Exod 19:13, 16, 19;
20:18.   Clouds as heavenly transport; Pal. Tg. Exod 19:4; 12:42.
303,104.265; 345,187.

1 Thess 5:19-20
See Neof. Gen 26:35 for extinguishing the spirit of concord and
charity; also Neof. Num.   138,183; 306.

2 Thess 2:8
Epiphany of Christ and revelation of the Messiah in the Pal. Tg.
267,246-52.

1 Tim 2:8
See Tg. Mal 1:11 on prayer. 186,289.

1 Tim 3:8
"Two tongues"; cf. Tg. Prv 28:23. 181,290.

1 Tim 3:15
"Column"; cf. Tg. Num 20:29. 234,48.

1 Tim 5:17-18
See Ps.-J. Deut 25:4; literal meaning extended. 201,161-66.

1 Tim 6:14
Epiphany of Christ and revelation of the Messiah in the Pal. Tg.
267,246-52.

2 Tim 1:10
Epiphany of Christ and the revelation of the Messiah in the Pal. Tg.
267,246-52.

2 Tim 3:8
Jannes and Jambres in Ps.-J. Exod 7:11; 1:15; Num 22:22. 267,
82-96; 235,55; 248,252; 138,156; 219; 265,106; 39,163; 158,55;
259,504-05; 6; 41; 234,45-46; 341,137; 230,230.

Titus 2:13
Epiphany of Christ and the revelation of the Messiah in the Pal. Tg.
267,246-52.

Titus 3:5
Creation; paschal background in Pal. Tg. 230,252.256.

Heb 1:6
See Tg. Exod 4:22; Hos 11:1; Gen 1:1. 241,28.

Heb 1:8
Cf. Tg. Ps 45:1-7. 95,8; 235,134.

Heb 2:2
See Neof. Exod 20:2, 3; Pal. Tg. Deut 33:2. 141,208; 303,294.

Heb 2:10
Self-cleansing Messiah and older form of Tg. Isa 53:10. 19,88.123.

Heb 3--4
Joshua-Jesus; cf. Tg. Josh 5. 239.

Heb 3:2-6
See Tg. 2 Sam 7:12-14; 1 Chr 17:10. Christ and Moses; cf. Tg.
Num 12:7. 80,236-37; 90,659.

Heb 4:6
Renewal, creation; paschal background of the Pal. Tg.   230,256.

Heb 5--7
Melchisedech in Jewish literature and Neof. Gen 14:18.   141,202-03;
138,166-67.

Heb 5:7
See Tg. Isa 53:4.   19,83.

Heb 5:8
Self-cleansing Messiah and older form of Tg. Isa 53:10.   19,88.123.

Heb 6:4
See Tg. Isa 9:1; Ps 18:29.   230,232-36.

Heb 7:25
Intercession; cf. Tg. Isa 53:12.   19,94.

Heb 9
See Tg. Exod 24:3-8.   303,151-52.

Heb 9:2
Showbread; cf. Onq., Ps.-J. Exod 25:30.   213,58 (ET:64).

Heb 9:12
Eternal redemption; see Ps.-J. Neof. m. Gen 49:18.   286,282.

Heb 9:15-17
Testament and alliance in Jewish thought.   234,35.

Heb 9:18, 22
Expiatory character of the blood of the covenant in Onq., Ps.-J.
Exod 24:8.   248,252; 272,128-29.

Heb 10:6
Citation of Ps 40:6 may reflect targumic usage.   272,97.

Heb 10:38-39
Tg. and Qumran on Hab 2:4.   347.

Heb 11:3
See Tg. Gen 49:1.   267,245.

Heb 11:4
Cain and Abel in Pal. Tg. Gen 4:8.   267,156-60; 138,164; 351; 224,
31-36; 130,134-36; 190.

Heb 11:13
See Neof. Gen 49:18; messianic expectations.   138,173.

Heb 11:17
"Beloved"; cf. love of Abraham in the Pal. Tg.   231,203-04.

Heb 11:17-19
Trial of faith, Abraham and Isaac in the Pal. Tg.   230,203.

Heb 11:18-19
Resurrection in the Pal. Tg. and Jewish tradition; cf. Tg. Gen 22.
230,205-06.

Heb 11:19
Isaac typology; see Tg. Lev 22:27.   257,255-56; 118,66-67.

Heb 11:31
Rahab, a model of faith in the Pal. Tg.   234,52.

Heb 12:24
Expiatory character of the blood of the covenant in Onq., Ps.-J.
Exod 24:8; cf. Neof. Gen 4:10.   248,252; 138,164; 224,31-36; 234,35.

Heb 13:13
"Going outside the camp" implies conversion to the Lord; cf. Ps.-J.
Exod 33:5-8.   267,180-81.

Heb 13:15
Spiritual sacrifices; cf. Ps.-J. Exod 40:6; Tg. Hos 14:3.   186,288.

Jas 1:16-18
New light and creation; paschal background in the Pal. Tg.   Favor
from above; cf. Neof., Frg. Gen 40:23.   230,256; 248,257.

Jas 2:21-23
See Frg. Gen 22:14; Ps.-J. Gen 15:6; 22:5; Frg. Gen 18:17; Isaac
typology and trial of faith.   208; 118,67; 230,203.

Jas 2:25
Rahab, model of faith in the Pal. Tgs.   234,52-53.

Jas 3:6
Inextinguishable fire; Neof. Gen 15:17; 28:25; 39:9; Neof. m. Gen
49:22.   138,178-79; 303,231.

Jas 5:11
See 11QtgJob.   248,285.

1 Pet 1:2
Expiatory character of the blood of the covenant in Onq., Ps.-J.
Exod 24:8.   248,252; 234,35.

1 Pet 1:3
Tgs. and Cain.   Regeneration and creation; paschal background in
the Pal. Tgs.   219; 230,256.

1 Pet 1:10-12
See Pal. Tg. Gen 28:11-12; 49:1.   132,77; 257,258; 251,215; 131,
339-40; 267,244-45; 286,134-35.278; 272,146-47.

1 Pet 1:13-19
Perfection of persons and of sacrificial animals; cf. Neof. Exod 12.
267,63.

1 Pet 1:17-18
Tg. Isa 56:1-9; 57:19 reflect Exod 21:1--22:23--*seder* and *haptara*.
Influence of synagogue readings.   299.

1 Pet 1:18-20
See Tg. Gen 22:8, 13; Isaac in the Pal. Tgs.   138,159-60; 251,202-03;
225; 234,31; 267,164-67; 249a,I 212.

1 Pet 1:23
Regeneration; paschal background in the Pal. Tgs.   230,256.

1 Pet 2:1-10
Pre-Christian Jewish tradition and stone-texts; cf. Tg. Isa 8:14;
28:1-21; Jer 51:26; Zech 4:7, 10; Ps 118:22.   323.

1 Pet 2:4-24
Tg. Isa 56:1-9; 57:19 reflect Exod 21:1--22:23--*seder* and *haptara*.
Influence of synagogue readings.   299.

1 Pet 2:4-8
Play on *bn* and *'bn*; cf. Onq. Gen 49:24; Tg. Ps 118:22.   238,28-29;
212,374-76; 95,11-14.

1 Pet 2:5
Expression for acceptable sacrifice found in Neof. Exod 29:18; Lev
1:9, 13, 17; 2:9; 3:5 etc.   248,255-56; 186,288.

1 Pet 2:9-10
Passover, illumination and liberation, Tg. Exod 12:42.   241,30;
230,256; 157,76-79; 272,105.

1 Pet 2:9
Disputed meaning of *basileion hierateuma*; cf. Tg. Exod 19:6; 1:21.
Also Tg. Isa 9:1; Ps 18:29.   272,148-56; 6,232; 230,232-36.

1 Pet 2:21-25
Plural for "sins." Isa 53:4, 12 at Qumran and in the Tgs.   295,
278-79.

1 Pet 3:20
Delay of punishment for repentance; see Neof. Gen 4:7; 18:21; Tg.
Hab 3:1.   303,171; 219; 234,67-68.

1 Pet 5:8
Cf. symbolism of the lion as the wicked king in the Tgs.   339,41-42.

2 Pet 1:17
Divine pleasure and targumic usage.   272,96-97.

2 Pet 1:19
Morning star and Tg. Num 24:17 messianic.   138,161; 341,165-66.

2 Pet 2:1
Pseudoprophets and pseudoteachers; cf. Neof. Num.   306.

2 Pet 2:4, 9, 10
Reserved for judgment; Neof. Gen 4:6-7.   138,178.

2 Pet 2:7
"Lot, the just" in Jewish tradition.   234,52.

2 Pet 2:15-16
Targumic evaluation of Balaam.   341,130.135.172; 138,160; 238,20;
284,60-65; 306; 267,168; 246,516.

2 Pet 3:7
Reserved for judgment; Neof. Gen 4:6-7.   138,178.

2 Pet 3:9
Delay of punishment for repentance; see Neof. Gen 4:7; 18:21; Tg.
Hab 3:1.   303,171; 234,67.

2 Pet 3:10-13
Cf. the theophany of Sinai in the Tgs.   303,243.

1 John 1:1
Memra of Yahweh in the Tgs.   137,381-94; 18; 286.

1 John 2:1-2
Expiatory intercession; cf. Tg. Job 33:24; Isa 53:12.   99a,385b;
19,94.

1 John 2:17
New order; paschal background in the Pal. Tgs.   230,253.

1 John 3:8-12
Cain and Abel in the Pal. Tg. Gen 4:8; 5:3.   267,156-60; 138,164;
224,31-36; 86,375; 131,342; 190; 115,79; 234,59-61; 130,134-36;
351; 104,132-41; 248,280-81; 106,45.179; 107,358; 132,79-80; 207.

Jude 6
Reserved for judgment; Neof. Gen 4:6-7.   138,178.

Jude 11-12
Targumic evaluation of Balaam and Cain. Verbs indicate punishment
and death. 341,130.135.172; 138,160.164; 351; 238,20; 284,60-65;
109,312; 218,267.273; 322,30; 224,30-36; 267,158-59; 246,516; 101.

Jude 14
Evidence for Aramaic use of Mara = Lord. 95,10-11.

Rev
Influence of the Pal. Tgs. in general. Rev and the paschal night
of the Tgs. 267,189-237; 235,166; 241,31-33.

Rev 1:4
Divine name and Ps.-J. Exod 3:14 and Deut 32:39. 267,97-117; 284,
77-78; 126,122-27.

Rev 1:6
Kingdom and priests; Tg. Exod 19:6; 1:21. 141,208; 238,27; 303,
54.218; 157,76-78.121-23; 267,227-30; 272,148-55; 6,232.

Rev 1:8
Divine name and Ps.-J. Exod 3:14 and Deut 32:39. 267,97-117; 284,
77-78; 126,122-27.

Rev 1:12, 16, 20
Seven lampstands and seven stars; Ps.-J. Exod 39:37; 40:4. 267,
192-99.

Rev 1:18
Keys in Frg. P V, Neof. Gen 30:22; Ps.-J. Deut 28:12. 238,17;
286,262-65.

Rev 2:7
"Tree of life"; paschal background in the Pal. Tgs. 267,254.

Rev 2:11
For second death, see Tg. Deut 33:6. 284,80-81; 267,117-25;
272,148.

Rev 2:14
The ungodly and the disciples of Balaam. 341,135.172; 238,20;
284,60-65; 267,168; 246,519.

Rev 2:17
Manna traditions in the Tgs. Ps.-J. Num 22:28: created after the
foundation of the world. Messianic wine preserved for the just.
141,208-09; 276,57-58.99-102; 249a,I 261.

Rev 3:12
"Column"; cf. Tg. Num 20:29. 234,48.

Rev 3:14

See Tg. Exod 4:22; Hos 11:1; Gen 1:1.   241,28.

Rev 4:2, 6

God enthroned above the sea; cf. Tg. Exod 15.   267,200-04.

Rev 4:7-9

Praise of living creatures; cf. Tg. Ezek 1:24.   303,187.

Rev 4:8

Divine name and Ps.-J. Exod 3:14 and Deut 32:39; cf. also Frg.,
Neof. Deut 32:3.   Kingship.   267,97-117.204-09; 126,122-27.

Rev 4:9

Divine acclamations.   267,214-17.

Rev 4:11

Kingship of the redeemer.   267,204-09.

Rev 5:5-6

Powerful and suffering Messiah; cf. Tg. Isa 53:8.   19,85.

Rev 5:6

Isaac typology; see Tg. Lev 22:27.   257,255-56.

Rev 5:7-14

Victory and kingship of the redeemer.   267,205-09.

Rev 5:7

God enthroned above the sea; cf. Tg. Exod 15.   267,199-209.

Rev 5:9-13

Song of Moses and the new song.   267,209-14.

Rev 5:10

Kingdom and priests; Tg. Exod 19:6.   238,27; 303,54.218; 157,76-78.
121-23; 267,227-30; 272,148-56; 6,232.

Rev 6:1-7

Tgs. introduce punishment into the text of the Ten Commandments;
cf. also Tg. Ezek 1:8.   303,100.185.

Rev 7:10

Victory and kingship of the redeemer.   267,205-09.

Rev 8:3, 4

Spiritual sacrifices; cf. Ps.-J. Exod 40:6; Tg. Hos 14:3.   186,288.

Rev 8:5

See Tg. Ezek 1:8.   303,185.

Rev 9:1-3

Hell as "well of the abyss"; cf. Neof. Gen 22:10.   138,179-80.

Rev 10:6
Delay of punishment for repentance; see Neof. Gen 4:7; 18:21; Tg.
Hab 3:1.   303,171.

Rev 10:8-11
Little scroll and ordeal of bitter waters; cf. Onq. Num 5 and Num
Rab. 9; see Rev 17--18.   176.

Rev 11:12
Cloud as heavenly transport, Pal. Tg. Exod 19:4; 12:42.   345,187.

Rev 11:17
Divine name and Ps.-J. Exod 3:14 and Deut 32:39.   267,97-117; 284,
77-78.

Rev 12
Targum references.   320; 267,222-26; 234,56; 248,263.

Rev 12:5
See Ps.-J. Exod 24:12.   303,155-62.

Rev 12:9-18
Serpent, creation and paschal background; cf. Pal. Tg. Gen 3:15.
138,174; 230,254; 234,56; 267,217-22; 25.

Rev 12:10
God enthroned above the sea; cf. Tg. Exod 15.   267,199-209.

Rev 12:17
See Pal. Tg. Gen 3:15.   267,217-22.

Rev 14:1-5
Song of Moses and the new song.   267,209-14.

Rev 15:1-4
Sea of glass and the liturgy of the book of Rev.   Song of Moses
and the new song.   267,201.209-14.

Rev 15:7
See Tg. Ezek 1:8.   303,185.

Rev 16:1
The "cup of wrath"; cf. Ps.-J. Gen 40:12.   249a,I 363.

Rev 16:5
See divine name in the Pal. Tg. Deut 32:39.   284,77-78; 267,101-12.

Rev 17--18
Little scroll and the ordeal of bitter waters; cf. Onq. Num 5 and
Num. Rab. 9; see Rev 10:8-11.   176.

Rev 17:8
See Tg. Isa 50:11.   221,5.

Rev 19:13, 15
Pal. Tg. Gen 49:11 and the messianism of Isa 63:1-6. 138,169; 197;
267,230-33; 248,264-65; 238; 32; 112,364; 284,55-56; 272,141.

Rev 19:13
Logos and the Memra of Yahweh in the Pal. Tgs.; e.g. Ps.-J. Exod
17:15. 86,370; 286,361; 137,381-94; 18.

Rev 19:15
Davidic messianism and the kingship of Jesus. 138,169; 195,28.

Rev 20:2
Serpent and creation. 138,175; 234,56.

Rev 20:6
Aramaic for "second death" only in Tg. Deut 33:6; see Tg. Exod
19:6; 1:21. 267,117-25; 284,80-81; 8,I 534; 303,54.226; 272,
123-24.148; 6,232.

Rev 20:7-10
On Gog and Magog, see Neof. Num 24:20; Ps.-J. Num 11:26. 138,175;
86,375-76; 306; 267,233-37.

Rev 20:11-15
Resurrection and creation; paschal background in the Pal. Tgs.
138,176-77; 230,254-55.

Rev 20:13
See Neof., Frg. Gen 30:22; Exod 15. 286,262-65.344.

Rev 20:14
Second death; cf. Tg. Deut 33:6; Isa 65:6, 16; 53:9. 267,117-25;
284,80-81; 8,I 534; 19,86-87; 272,148.

Rev 21:1-5
Paschal background in the Pal. Tgs. 230,254-55.

Rev 21:1
See Pal. Tg. Deut 32:1; Ps.-J. Exod 15:19; 14:9. 284,78-79; 230,
231.

Rev 21:2
New Jerusalem as bride; see Pal. Tg. Gen 3:24. 286,171.

Rev 21:3
Emmanuel and creation, paschal background in the Pal. Tgs. 230,257.

Rev 21:8
Second death; cf. Tg. Deut 33:6; also Isa 65:6, 15; 53:9. 267,
117-25; 284,80-81; 8,I 534; 19,86-87.

Rev 21:23
New creation; paschal background in the Pal. Tgs.   230,255.

Rev 22:1-2
Wells and sources of living water in the Tgs., esp. Tg. Isa 55:1-13
(?).   330; 331.

Rev 22:2
Karpon poiein a Hebrew and Aramaic idiom; cf. Tg. Gen 1:11, 12;
Jer 17:8.   Paschal background for the tree of life.   92,138-39;
231,254.

Rev 22:16
Star of Num 24:17 messianic in Ps.-J. and Frg.   341,165; 138,161.

Baptism. Circumcision in Judaism; Tg. Exod 4:25-26. Baptism and passover; Tg. Exod 12:42. 338; 339; 30; 241,32.

Church. An assembly of priests; see esp. Tg. Exod 19:6. A kingly people. 303,218-30.

Cloud Traditions. Traditions in OT, Judaism, and the NT. 256.

Eucharist. Targumists exclude the sprinkling of the people and the sacrificial meal from the covenant; not so NT eucharistic texts. 81.

Eschatology. Individual and collective in Tgs. and NT: see Ps.-J. Gen 25:28; Neof. Gen 25:34; 4:8. Fear of retribution: Neof. Gen 22:10. Salvation; Neof. Gen 15:1; 22:10. Cloud symbolism. Renovation of the world; cf. Tg. Hab 3:2. General. 138,175-76. 179-81; 256; 303,172; 30; 272,133-41.

Flesh. Ethical connotations of *sarx* in Tg. Gen 6:3 in contrast to the spirit of God. 248,257-59; 132,78-79; 131,341-42; 286,186.

Glory. Targum substitutions for the divine name in the NT. 248, 273; 272,98-101.

Healing and Laying on of Hands. Not in OT, but in Jewish tradition and the Gospels. 343,115.

Intercession. Developments in Jewish concept of intercession and intercessors prior to the NT. 243.

Isaac and the Akedah; NT Theology of Redemption. 267,164-68; 230,202-12; 248,271-72; 360; 138,162-63.181-82; 351,126; 201, 81-82; 257,255-56; 241,36-40; 212,380-85; 118; 250,268-72; 29; 206; 228; 325; 340.

Judgment. Belief in the last judgment in the Pal. Tg. Gen 3:19; Neof. Gen 4:6-7. Judgment and repentance; Tg. Hab 3. 138,177-78; 248,287; 303,174-82.

Justification. See Pal. Tg. Gen 4:8-11. 130,134-36.

Kingdom. "Kingdom," "house," "community" in the Tgs. of the Nathan prophecy; local sense of kingdom in the NT. 80.

Lamb. Conquering lamb of Rev and Pharaoh's dream; Ps.-J. Exod
1:15. 220; 108.

Law in Judaism. 274.

Laying on of Hands and Healing. Not in the OT, but in Jewish
tradition and the Gospels. 343,115.

Man. Created red, brown, and white; Pal. Tg. Gen 2:7. 121,54.

Mary. Jewish traditions about Miryam may throw light on NT Marian
texts. 231.

Messiah. Doctrine of the Messiah in the Tgs. Pal. Tg. Exod 12:42
and the coming of the Messiah. Pre-Christian messianic interpretation of stone texts. Targumic interpretation of Gen 3:15. 267,
13-14.238-46; 241,33-36; 95; 220; 144; 13; 251,168-70; 345,137-40.
97-98.158.171; 284,88-90; 154; 30; 19; 28,59-96.315; 106,65-74;
252; 195; 6,275; 256,202-08; 157,25-28; 17,104-07; 25.

Palestinian Targums and the Gospels. 267,126-49.256.

Palestinian Targums and Paul. 267,254-55.

Palestinian Targums and Revelation. 267,189-223.255-56.

Passion Narratives. Rules of Tgs. and passion chronology; see Tg.
Lev 24:12; Num 9:8; 15:34; 27:5; compare the texts of Neof., Frg.,
and Ps.-J. 211.

Passover. Study of Neof. Exod 12:42. Moses' traditions and a new
exodus. 229; 230; 141,207; 241; 6.

Pentecost. Feast of Weeks in the Tgs. as feast of Covenant and
Law; Pal. Tg. Exod 19--20; 24. 248,260; 141,207-08; 303; 227.

Redemption. Value of the merits of the just; Neof. Gen 12:3;
18:18; 26:24. Akedah and the atonement. For a comparison with
the redemption from Egypt, see Neof. Lev 19:2; 25:3-8; Neof. m.
Lev 11:44-45. 138,181-82; 243; 116; 286,407; 6; 241.

Resurrection. Resurrection in the Tgs.; e.g. Tg. Hos 6:2, 3;
Neof. Gen 19:26; Frg. Exod 13:17; Frg., Neof. Gen 4:8; Neof.,
Ps.-J. Gen 3:19; Ps.-J. Exod 20:18; Tg. Hab 3. 360,588; 138,
176-77; 146,35.76.80.175.241-42; 248,287.

Retribution. Rewards and punishment in the world to come; Neof.
Gen 4:7; 15:17; 28:25; 39:9; Neof. m. Gen 49:22. 138,178-79.

Servant. Servant in Tg. Isa 53. 121,275.

Son of God and monogenēs in the NT. See Neof. Gen 1:1. Notion of
divine sonship weakened in Tgs.; cf. Tg. Pss 2:7; 89:28; 80:16;
2 Sam 7:14. 138,174; 255,88-89; 27,247.

Son of Man. Targum usage and messianic sense. 348; 236,397-99; 105; 318,433; 172,93; 171,296-97; 28,312; 12.

Spirit. "Spirit of holiness" in the Tgs. and Holy Spirit in the NT. Spirit in creation in the Tgs. Spirit and sanctification; Tg. Ezek 1:3. Spirit and Church. General. 138,172-73; 141, 206-07; 251,45; 86,367; 137,394-96; 135,232-33; 121,189-90.206; 256,234-45; 272,107-14.

Water (Living). The well traditions and the Law in the Tgs. 248, 274-77.

Word of God. The Memra of Yahweh in the Tgs. as creating and revealing, and the Logos of John. 138,170-72; 92,298-99; 21, 458-59; 141,205-06; 303,245-79; 86,366; 286; 26; 18; 107,523-24; 271; 272,98-106.

APPENDIX
RECENT EDITIONS OF THE TARGUMS AND TRANSLATIONS

Targums of the Pentateuch

BERLINER, A. *Targum Onkelos* (London, Berlin, Frankfurt a. M.:
Nutt, Gorzelanczyk, Kauffmann, 1884; reprint Jerusalem: Makor,
1974).
- Erster Theil: Text, nach editio Sabioneta 1557;
- Zweiter Theil: Noten, Einleitung und Register.

SPERBER, A. *The Bible in Aramaic Based on Old Manuscripts and
Printed Texts*. Vol. I. *The Pentateuch according to Targum
Onkelos* (Leiden: Brill, 1959).

*Targum Onkelos to the Pentateuch. A Collection of Fragments in
the Library of the Jewish Theological Seminary of America, New
York.* Introductory Remarks by Daniel Boyarin (Jerusalem:
Makor, 1976) 4 vols. Facsimile edition.

GINSBURGER, M. *Pseudo-Jonathan (Thargum Jonathan ben Usiël zum
Pentateuch). Nach der Londoner Handschrift* (Brit. Mus. add.
27031) (Berlin: S. Calvary, 1903; reprint Hildesheim: Olms,
1971; Jerusalem: Makor, 1974).

RIEDER, D. *Pseudo-Jonathan. Targum Jonathan ben Uziel on the
Pentateuch copied from the London MS.* (British Museum add.
27031) (Jerusalem: Salomon's Printing Press, 1974).

GINSBURGER, M. *Das Fragmententhargum (Thargum jeruschalmi zum
Pentateuch)* (Berlin: S. Calvary, 1899; reprint Jerusalem:
Makor, 1974).
- Editio princeps: Biblia Rabbinica de Bomberg (Venice, 1517)
collated with Leipzig 1 and Vat. 440.

DÍEZ MACHO, A. "Un nuevo manuscrito del Targum fragmentario,"
Homenaje a Juan Prado (edd. L. Alvarez Verdes y E. J. Alonso
Hernandez, Madrid: CSIC, 1975) 533-51.
- A study of MS. 6684, National and University Library of
Jerusalem.

KLEIN, M. "The Extant Sources of the Fragmentary Targum to the
Pentateuch," *HUCA* 46 (1975) 115-37.

DÍEZ MACHO, A. *Biblia Polyglotta Matritensia*. Series IV:
Targum Palaestinense in Pentateuchum. Adduntur Targum Pseudo-
jonathan, Targum Onkelos, et Targum Palaestinensis hispanica
versio. 5: *Deuteronomium* Caput I. Editio critica curante A. Díez
Macho (Matriti: CSIC, 1965).

129

Biblia Polyglotta IV. *Targum Palaestinense in Pentateuchum.* L. 4.
    Numeri (Matriti: CSIC, 1977).

DÍEZ MACHO, A. *Neophyti 1. Targum Palestinense MS de la Biblioteca
    Vaticana*

    - Tomo I. Génesis. Edición Príncipe, Introducción General y
    Versión Castellana. Traducciones Cotejadas de la Version
    Castellana: Francesa: R. LeDéaut; Inglesa: Martin McNamara y
    Michael Maher (Madrid, Barcelona: CSIC, 1968).

    - Tomo II. Exodo. Edición Príncipe, Introducción y Versión
    Castellana. Traducciones Cotejadas de la Versión Castellana:
    Francesa: R. LeDéaut; Inglesa: Martin McNamara y Michael
    Maher. Lugares Paralelos a la Haggadá del Génesis de Pseudo-
    jonatán y Neophyti 1: Etan B. Levine (Madrid, Barcelona:
    CSIC, 1970).

    - Tomo III. Levítico. Edición Príncipe, Introducción y Versión
    Castellana. Traducciones Cotejadas de la Versión Castellana:
    Francesa: R. LeDéaut; Inglesa: Martin McNamara y Michael
    Maher. Lugares Paralelos a Exodo y Levítico de Pseudojonatán
    y Neophyti 1: Etan B. Levine. El Memra de Yahweh en el MS
    Neophyti 1: Domingo Muñoz (Madrid, Barcelona: CSIC, 1971).

    - Tomo IV. Números. Edición Príncipe, Introducción y Versión
    Castellana. Traducciones Cotejadas de la Versión Castellana:
    Francesa: R. LeDéaut; Inglesa: Martin McNamara. Lugares
    Paralelos a Números de Pseudojonatán y Neophyti 1: Etan B.
    Levine (Madrid: CSIC, 1974).

    - Tomo V. Deuteronomio. Edición Príncipe, Introducción y
    Versión Castellana. Traducciones Cotejadas de la Versión
    Castellana: Francesa: R. LeDéaut, Inglesa: Martin McNamara y
    Michael Maher. Lugares Paralelos a Deuteronomio de Pseudo-
    jonatán y Neophyti 1: Etan B. Levine (Madrid, CSIC, 1978).

Cairo Geniza Fragments

KAHLE, P. *Masoreten des Westens II* (Stuttgart: Kohlhammer, 1930;
    reprint Hildesheim: Olms, 1967).

    - MS A (7th - 8th cent.): Exod 21:1--22:27;
    - MS E (8th cent.): Gen 6:18--7:15; 9:5-23; 28:17--31:35;
            38:16--39:10; 41:6-26 ; 43:23--44:5;
    - MSS B C D (9th cent.): B - Gen 4:4-16:
                             C - Gen 31:38-54; 32:13-30; 34:9-25;
                                   35:7-15;

                         D - Gen 7:17--8:9; 37:20-34; 38:16-26;
                             43:7-18; 43:20--44:23; 48:11-20;
                             Exod 5:20--6:10; 7:10-22; 9:21-23;
                             Deut 5:19-26; 26:18--27:11; 28:15-18,
                             27-29;
- MS F (10th - 11th cent.): Lev 22:26--23:44; Num 28:16-25;
                             Exod 19:1--20; 23; Num 28:26-31;
                             Deut 34:5-12 (festive readings);
- MS G (10th - 11th cent.): Fragments of poetic compositions
                             on Exod 15 and 20.

GINSBURGER, M. "Neue Fragmente des Thargum jeruschalmi," *ZDMG* 58
(1904) 374-78.
- Fragments of Deut 1--5.

DÍEZ MACHO, A. "Nuevos fragmentos del Targum Palestinense," *Sef*
15 (1955) 31-39 (Kahle's MS E).
- E. N. Adler Collection MS 2755 f. 2: Gen 37:15-33;
                                  f. 1: Gen 40:5-18;
- E. N. Adler Collection MS 2578 ff. 21-22: Gen 41:43-57;
                                  42:34--43:10.

BAARS, W. "A Targum on Exod. XV 7-21 from the Cairo Geniza," *VT*
11 (1961) 340-42.
- Bodl. MS Hebr f. 102, f.5.

GRELOT, P. "Une Tosephta targoumique sur Genèse XXII dans un
manuscrit liturgique de la Geniza du Caire," *REJ* 116 (1957) 5-26.
- Gen 22:5-9.

RUEGER, H. "Ein neues Genesis-Fragment mit komplizierter baby-
lonischer Punktuation aus der Kairo-Geniza," *VT* 13 (1963)
235-37.
- MS T.-S. K. 25.129, University Library, Cambridge: Gen 3:24--
4:5; Gen 4:7-12.

DÍEZ MACHO, A. "Un Nuevo MS. 'Palestinense' del Libro de Jueces
entre los Fragmentos de la Genizah de la Biblioteca Universitaria
de Cambridge (T.-S. New Series 281^2)," *Sef* 23 (1963) 236-51.
- Judg 8:30--9:48.

DÍEZ MACHO, A. "Deux nouveaux fragments du Targum palestinien à
New York," *Studi sull'Oriente e la Bibbia offerti al P. G.
Rinaldi* (Genova: Studio e Vita, 1967) 175-89.
- MS 605 ff. 6-7, Jewish Theological Seminary = Kahle's MS F:
Exod 14:13-14; 14:29--15:1; 17:15-16; 19:1-8;
- MS 501 f. 1, Jewish Theological Seminary = Kahle's MS B:
Gen 2:17--3:6.

DÍEZ MACHO, A. "Nuevo manuscrito bíblico 'palestinense' procedente
de la Genizah de El Cairo," *SPap* 6 (1967) 15-25.

- 2 Chr 13:16-20; 14:4-8; 14:14--15:6; 15:13-17.

DÍEZ MACHO, A. *MS Neophyti 1.* Tomo I. Génesis (Madrid, Barcelona:
CSIC, 1968) 113 y Cuadro Synoptico I.

- MS 4017, Bibliothèque Nationale et Universitaire de Strasbourg =
Kahle's MS F: Exod 19:25--20:13.

DÍEZ MACHO, A. *Manuscritos hebreos y arameos de la Biblia* (Studia
Ephemeridis "Augustinianum"; Rome: Institutum Patristicum
"Augustinianum," 1971) 217-20.

- MS T.-S. N. S. 76, Cambridge University Library = Kahle's MS
D: Gen 41:32-42.

DÍEZ MACHO, A. "Nuevos fragmentos de Tosefta targumica," *Sef* 16
(1956) 313-24.

- Jewish Theological Seminary, MS 605 f. 30ab: Exod 20:2-3, 7-8;
MS T.-S. B 12_2: Gen 44:18.

FUSTE ARA, R. "El fragmento targúmico T.-S. B 3 de la Biblioteca
Universitaria de Cambridge (En torno a los MSS. yemeníes),"
EstBíb 15 (1956) 85-94.

- Num 24:22-25; 25; 26:1-43.

DÍEZ MACHO, A. "Fragmento de una nueva recensión del Targum Jonatán
ben ^{C}Uzziel a los Profetas (T.-S. B 12_1)," *Sef* 16 (1956) 405-06.

- 1 Kgs 2:3-5.

The Samaritan Targum

BRUELL, A. *Das samaritanische Targum zum Pentateuch.* Zum erstenmal
in hebraeischer Quadratschrift (Frankfurt a. M.: W. Erras, 1873-7!
reprint Hildesheim: Olms, 1971).

MACDONALD, J. *Memar Marqah. The Teaching of Marqah.* With an
English translation. 2 vols. (BZAW 84; Berlin: Töpelmann, 1963).

DÍAZ FERNÁNDEZ, J. R. "Ediciones del Targum samaritano," *EstBíb*
15 (1956) 105-08.

DÍAZ FERNÁNDEZ, J. R. "Los fragmentos del Targum samaritano publicad(
EstBíb 15 (1956) 297-300.

- Notices only.

The Targum of the Prophets

DE LAGARDE, P. *Prophetae Chaldaice* (Leipzig: Teubner, 1872; reprint
Osnabrück: Zeller, 1967).

STENNING, J. *The Targum of Isaiah.* Edited with a translation
(Oxford: Clarendon, 1949).

SPERBER, A. *The Bible in Aramaic Based on Old Manuscripts and
Printed Texts* Vol. II. The Former Prophets according to Targum
Jonathan (Leiden: Brill, 1959). Vol. III. The Latter Prophets

according to Targum Jonathan (Leiden: Brill, 1962).

FEIGON, G. *Yemenite Targum Manuscript to the Twelve Minor Prophets* (Enelow Memorial Collection at the Jewish Theological Seminary 27; San Diego: Bureau of Jewish Education, 1971).

DÍEZ MACHO, A. *Targum to the Former Prophets. Codex New York 229 from the Library of the Jewish Theological Seminary of America.* Introductory Remarks (38 pp. in Hebrew). Facsimile Edition (Jerusalem: Makor, 1974).

FLORIT, J. *Biblia Babilonica. Profetas Posteriores* (Targum) (Salamanca: Verona, 1977).

- MSS published. The nucleus of a doctoral dissertation presented at the University of Barcelona.

Fragments of Palestinian Targums of the Prophets (see also Geniza Fragments)

DE LAGARDE, P. *Prophetae Chaldaice* (Leipzig: Teubner, 1872; reprint Osnabrück: Zeller, 1967) 128-30.

- Marginalia of Codex Reuchlinianus.

BACHER, A. "Kritische Untersuchungen zum Prophetentargum," *ZDMG* 28 (1974) 1-72 esp. 4-22.

STENNING, J. *The Targum of Isaiah.* Edited with a translation (Oxford: Clarendon, 1949) 224-28 = De Lagarde.

DÍEZ MACHO, A. "Un nuevo Targum a los Profetas," *EstBíb* 15 (1956) 287-95.

- MS 607 (ENA 2576, f. 5ab): Josh 5:5--6:1.

DÍEZ MACHO, A. "Un segundo fragmento del Targum palestinense a los Profetas," *Bib* 39 (1958) 198-205.

- Pentateuch of Salonica, Schocken Library, Jerusalem: Ezek 37:1-14.

SPERBER, A. *The Bible in Aramaic* II (1959) ix-x *(sigla)*.

SPERBER, A. *The Bible in Aramaic* III (1962) x-xi *(sigla)*;
- 23-25: Isa 10:32-33;
  462-65: Hab 3:1--5:11;
  479-80: Zech 2:14-15.

The Targums of the Hagiographa

DE LAGARDE, P. *Hagiographa Chaldaice* (Leipzig: Teubner, 1873; reprint Osnabrück: Zeller, 1967).

SPERBER, A. *The Bible in Aramaic Based on Old Manuscripts and Printed Texts* Vol. IV A. The Hagiographa. Transition from Translation to Midrash (Chronicles, Ruth, Canticles, Lamentations, Ecclesiastes, Esther) (Leiden: Brill, 1968).

MELAMED, R. H. *The Targum to Canticles according to Six Yemen MSS.*
compared with the 'Textus Receptus' as contained in De Lagarde's
'Hagiographa Chaldaice' (Philadelphia: Dropsie College, 1921).
LE DÉAUT, R., ROBERT, J. *Targum des Chroniques* (Cod. Vat. Urb.
Ebr. 1) Tome I. Introduction et traduction. Tome II. Texte
et glossaire (AnBib 51; Rome: Pontifical Biblical Institute, 1971)
LEVINE, E. *The Aramaic Version of Ruth* (AnBib 58; Rome: Pontifical
Biblical Institute, 1973).
- Text, English translation, analysis and commentary.
LEVINE, E. *The Aramaic Version of Jonah* (Jerusalem: Jerusalem
Academic Press, 1975).
- Introduction, text, English translation and commentary.
LEVINE, E. *The Aramaic Version of Lamentations* (New York: Hermon,
1976).
LEVINE, E. *The Targum to the Five Megillot. Ruth, Ecclesiastes,*
Canticles, Lamentations, Esther. Codex Vat. Urb. I. Facsimile
edition. Introductory Note, translations (English) and indices
(Jerusalem: Makor, 1977).
SULZBACH, A. *Targum Scheni zum Buch Esther* (Frankfurt a. M.:
Kaufmann, 1920).

The Qumran Targums
VAN DER PLOEG, J., VAN DER WOUDE, A. *Le Targum de Job de la grotte*
XI de Qumrân. Edité et traduit ... (Koninklijke Nederlandse
Akademie van Wetenschaffen; Leiden: Brill, 1971).
- Job 37:10--42:17; fragments of 17:14--26:33.
SOKOLOFF, M. *The Targum to Job from Qumran Cave XI* (Bar-Ilan Studies
in Near Eastern Languages and Culture; Ramat-Gan: Bar-Ilan
University, 1974).
- Text, English translation, commentary, morphology, and glossary.
JONGELING, B., LABUSCHAGNE, C., VAN DER WOUDE, A. *Aramaic Texts*
from Qumran. With translations and annotations. Vol. I (Leiden:
Brill, 1976).
- Tg. Job, GenAp, Prayer of Nabonidus.
Discoveries in the Judaean Desert VI. Qumran Grotte 4 II. I.
Archéologie par R. de Vaux avec les contributions de J. W. B. Barn
et J. Carswell. II. Tefillin, Mezuzot et Targums (4Q128-4Q157)
par J. T. Milik (Oxford: Clarendon, 1977).
- 86-89: Tg. Lev 16:12-15, 18-21;
  90: Tg. Job 3:4-5; 4:16--5:4.

Targumic Toseptas

MERX, A. *Chrestomathia Targumica* (Berlin: Reuther, 1888).

EPSTEIN, A. "Tosefta du Targoum Jerouschalmi," *REJ* 30 (1895) 44-51.

GINSBURGER, M. *Das Fragmententhargum* (Berlin: S. Calvary, 1899)
  71-74.
  - Gen 4:7, 8, 23; 38:26; 44:18; 49:18.

SPERBER, A. *The Bible in Aramaic* I (1959) xvii-xviii, 354-57.

GRELOT, P. "Une tosephta targoumique sur Zacharie II, 14-15," *RB*
  73 (1966) 197-211.

GRELOT, P. "Deux tosephtas targoumiques inédites sur Isaïe LXVI,"
  RB 79 (1972) 511-43.

GRELOT, P. "A propos d'une tosephta targoumique," *RB* 80 (1973) 363.
  - A textual correction of Tg. Isa 66:23 on p. 538 of the previous
  article.

KASHER, R. "The Targumic Additions to the Haphtara for the Shabbath
  of Hannuka," *Tarb* 45 (1976) 27-45 (in Hebrew).
  - Addition to Zech 2:14--4:7; cf. *JSJ* 8 (1977) 124-25.

KLEIN, M. "The Targumic Tosefta to Exodus 15:2," *JJS* 26 (1975)
  61-67.
  - Biblioteca Palatina di Parma, Codice de Rossi 2887 (736) f.
  38ab.

Other Targum Manuscripts (published or partly published or noted)

FELMAN, M. *Critical Edition of a Yemenite Manuscript of the Targum
  to Isaiah.* Dissertation Yeshiva University, 1949.

DÍEZ MACHO, A., LARRAYA, J. "El MS 4084 ff. 1-11 de la Biblioteca
  Nacional y Universitaria de Estraburgo. Un largo fragmento del
  Targum de Jonatan ben ᶜUzziel en texto babilonico," *EstBíb* 19
  (1960) 75-90; 361-68.
  - Judg 21:22-25; 1 Sam 1:1-17; 1:18--2:8; 2:8--3:12; 2 Sam 18:19--
  20:2; 20:1--23:4.

DÍEZ MACHO, A. "Un MS. de Onqelos de transición del sistema
  palestinense al prototiberiense: MS 607, ENA 2576, del Seminario
  Teológico Judío di New York (Onqelos Gen 4:7--6:1)," *EstE* 34
  (1960) 461-66.

DÍEZ MACHO, A., LARRAYA, J., "El MS. 4083 f.9 de la Biblioteca
  Nacional y Universitaria de Estraburgo (Fragmento de Amós 1:8--
  3:7, en hebreo y targum babilónicos)," *EstBíb* 19 (1960) 91-95.

DÍEZ MACHO, A. "A Yemenite Manuscript for the Edition of Babylonian
  Onqelos. MS. 133a (E. N. Adler Catalogue 1705) of the Jewish
  Theological Seminary of New York," *OrAnt* 6 (1967) 215-20.
  - Onq. Deut 28:15-51.

DÍEZ MACHO, A. "A Fundamental Manuscript for an Edition of the
    Babylonian Onqelos to Genesis: MS 152 of the Jewish Theological
    Seminary of New York," *In Memoriam Paul Kahle* (edd. M. Black,
    G. Fohrer; BZAW 103; Berlin: Töpelmann, 1968) 62-78.
    - Transcription of Gen 39.
DÍEZ MACHO, A. "Manuscritos babilónicos de la Biblia procedentes
    del Yemen. II Textos arameos," *AugRom* 9 (1969) 427-54.
    - MS 153 (EMC 48): Exod 3:22--8:15 (Tg.);
      MS 240 (EMC 73): Isa 35:9--38:11; 40:20-27; 42:21; 43:3-12
      (Hebr., Tg., Arab.)
DÍEZ MACHO, A., DE J. MARTÍNEZ, T., "MS. 4065, pp. 83-84, de la
    Biblioteca Nacional y Universitaria de Estraburgo (Nuevo
    fragmento del Targum de Onqelos en texto babilónico)," *EstBíb*
    19 (1960) 245-47.
    - Exod 26:17--27:3
DÍEZ MACHO, A., DE J. MARTÍNEZ, T. "MS. 4065 pp. 81-82 de la
    Biblioteca Universitaria de Estrasburgo (Nuevo fragmento
    babilónico del Exodo)," *EstBíb* 17 (1958) 429-36.
    - Hebrew and Onqelos of Exod 3:12--4:9.
DÍEZ MACHO, A. "Nuevos manuscritos bíblicos babilónicos," *EstBíb*
    16 (1957) 235-77.
    - Description of several MSS and publication of Hebrew and Aramaic
      of Judg 7:17-24; 7:5-9; 7:13; 7:2-5; 6:30-34; 6:26-29.
DÍEZ MACHO, A. "Fragmento del texto hebreo y arameo del libro de
    Números escrito en una muy antigua Měgil.la en el sistema
    babilónico (MS ENA 3781 [40] del Seminario Teológico Judío de
    Nueva York)," *Sef* 17 (1957) 386-88.
    - Hebrew and Onqelos of Num 32:25-33.
DÍEZ MACHO, A. "Manuscritos babilónicos de la Biblia procedentes
    del Yemen. I Textos hebreos y arameos," *AugRom* 9 (1969) 197-234.
DÍEZ MACHO, A. "Importants manuscrits hébreux et araméens aux
    Etats-Unis," VTSup 4 (Leiden: Brill, 1957) 27-46.
    - Notices only; for Targums, cf. esp. pp. 38-40.
DÍEZ MACHO, A. "A new fragment of Isaiah with Babylonian pointing,"
    Textus I (Jerusalem, 1960) 132-43.
    - Hebrew text only is reproduced without the accompanying Targum.
DÍEZ MACHO, A. "Nuevos manuscritos importantes bíblicos o litúrgicos
    en hebreo o arameo," *Sef* 16 (1956) 1-22.
    - Notices only; no texts published.
KOMLOS, Y. "Nosaḥ ha-Targum ᶜal qerīᶜat Yam-Sūf," *Sinai* 45 (1959)
    223-28.
KOMLOS, Y. "Kitbe yad šel Targumim," *Sinai* 44 (1958) 467-81.

Other Translations (not included in the above editions)

Latin: WALTON, B. *Bibliorum Sacrorum* (London: Roycroft, 1653-57)
          I: Onqelos. II: Jonathan of the Former Prophets; Ruth;
          Esther; III: Job; Psalms; Proverbs; Ecclesiastes; Jonathan
          of the Latter Prophets; IV: Pseudo-Jonathan and Fragmentary
          Targum.

English: ETHERIDGE, J. *The Targums of Onkelos and Jonathan ben
          Uzziel on the Pentateuch with the Fragments of the
          Jerusalem Targum from the Chaldee* 2 vols. (London:
          Green Longman, and Roberts, 1862-65; reprint New York:
          Ktav, 1968).

          GREENUP, A. *The Targum on the Book of Lamentations,
          translated* (Sheffield, 1893).

          GROSSFELD, B. (Editor) *The Targum to the Five Megilloth*
          (New York: Hermon, 1973). A collection of older transla-
          tions.

          BOWKER, J. *The Targums and Rabbinic Literature*
          (Cambridge: University Press, 1969) 93-297. A partial
          translation of Pseudo-Jonathan Targum of Genesis.

German: ALTSCHUELER, M. *Die aramaeische Bibel-Versionen*
          (Targumim). *Targum Jonathan Ben Uzij'el und Targum
          Jerusalemij, Text, Umschrift und Uebersetzung* (Orbis
          Antiquitatum; Wien, Leipzig: Lumen, 1909). Pars I, Tom.
          I. Vol. I: Genesis.

Italian: PIATELLI, A. *Targum Shir ha-Shirim* (Parafrasi aramaico
          del Cantico dei Cantici) (Rome: Barulli, 1975). Transla-
          tion and notes.

French: LE DÉAUT, R., ROBERT, J. *Targum du Pentateuque.* Traduc-
          tion des deux recensions palestiniennes complètes avec
          introduction, paralèles, notes et index. Tome I. Genèse
          (SC 245; Paris: Cerf, 1978). Tome II. Exode-Lévitique.
          Tome III. Nombres-Deutéronome (in preparation).

Dutch: MULDER, M. J. *De targum op het Hooglied. Inleiding,
          vertaling en korte verklaring* (Exegetica, Nieuwe reeks 4;
          Amsterdam: Ton Bolland, 1975).

          JONGELING, B. *Een Aramees Bock Job.* (Exegetica, Nieuwe
          reeks 3; Amsterdam: Ton Bolland, 1974).
          - Translation of 11QtgJob.